LIVING TRADITIONS

LIVING TRADITIONS

A CELEBRATION OF JEWISH LIFE

ITZIK BECHER

MALLARD PRESS

A FRIEDMAN GROUP BOOK

Published by MALLARD PRESS
An Imprint of BDD Promotional Book Company, Inc.
666 Fifth Avenue
New York, N.Y. 10103

Mallard Press and the accompanying duck logo are registered trademarks of the BDD Promotional Book Company, Inc. registered in the U.S. Patent and Trademark Office.

Copyright © 1993 by Michael Friedman Publishing Group, Inc.

First published in the United States of America in 1993 by The Mallard Press.

ISBN 0-7924-5539-8

LIVING TRADITIONS
A *Celebration of Jewish Life*
was prepared and produced by
Michael Friedman Publishing Group, Inc.
15 West 26th Street
New York, New York 10010

Editors: Stephen Williams and Kelly Matthews
Art Director: Jeff Batzli
Design: Jules Perlmutter
Photography Editor: Ede Rothaus

Typeset by Bookworks Plus
Color separations by Rainbow Graphic Arts Co., Ltd.
Printed and bound in Hong Kong by Leefung-Asco Printers Co., Ltd.

DEDICATION

To my wife, Pnina, whose new traditions have infused my old ones with life. And to my father, Gershon-Henokh, who can no longer see how his own ways have woven into my path.

CONTENTS

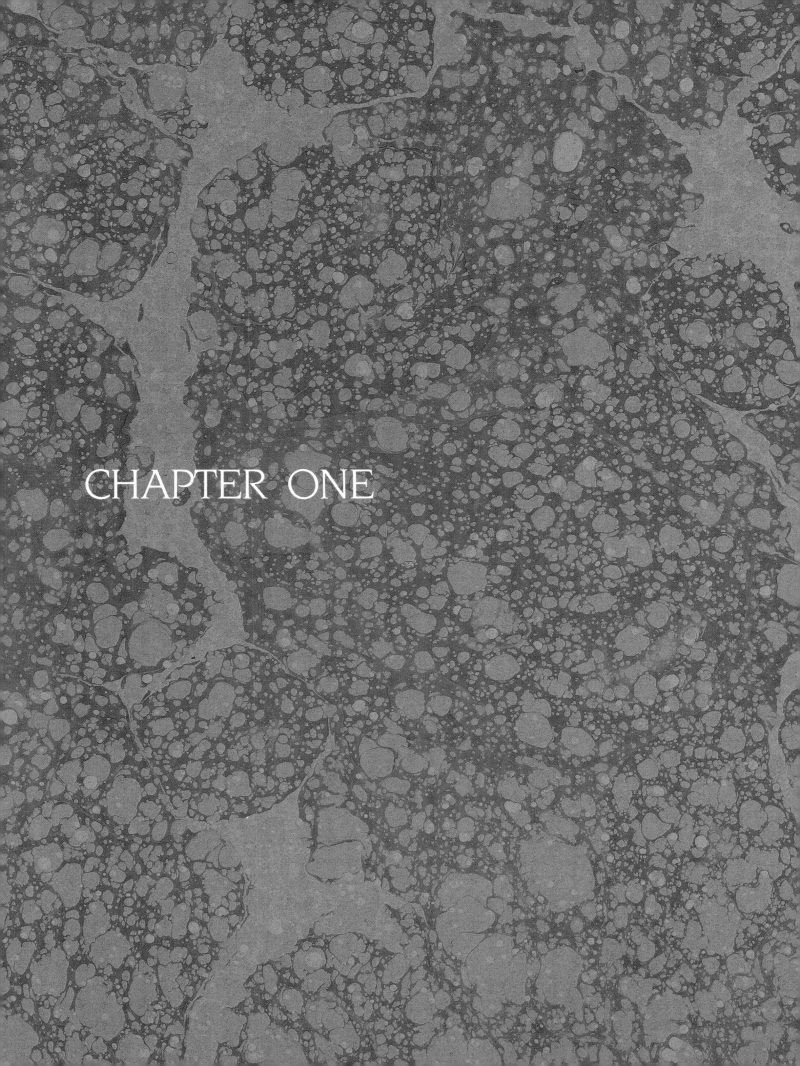

CHAPTER ONE

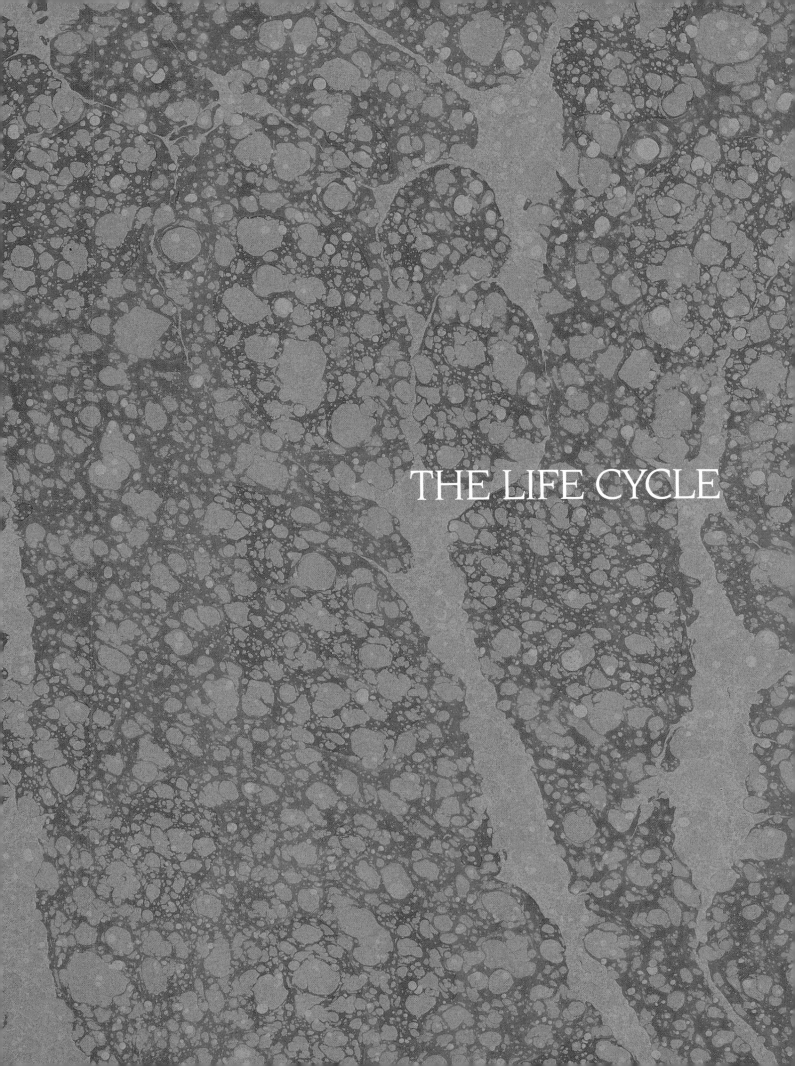

THE LIFE CYCLE

IN THE BEGINNING

Birth

Excitement. First cry of life. First breath of air. First human touch. A baby is born. "Guard and protect this father and mother and may they live to rear their child in the fear of God, study of the Torah, for the wedding canopy, and for the life of good deeds," says the blessing, the core of the Jewish life cycle. A soul is introduced into the world. It is the first step on the long path of a Jew: birth, bar or bat mitzvah, marriage, childbirth, and death.

Ancient Jewish societies were exposed to great dangers. The newborn and his mother had to be protected from all possible evil, which gave rise to an impressive catalog of folk traditions and folklore. Some of these rituals have remained unchanged for centuries, while others have reemerged in different forms. Some are reasonable; others seem strange and incomprehensible.

The protective rituals begin before birth. Almost from the very moment of conception, an expectant Jewish mother and her family protect the precious baby-to-come from the terrible Lilith (in Jewish lore, a female evil spirit, Adam's first wife). Some pregnant mothers pray at their family's grave to ensure a safe delivery. Some families draw a magic chalk-circle around the labor bed; others like to blow the *shofar* (ram's horn) in the delivery room. Some give the baby a code name so that evil Lilith will not recognize it. In the past, when a delivery was difficult and lasted a long time, the family opened all the windows and doors of the house to release tension. Future Jewish parents, prepared for the worst, rarely buy clothing, furniture, and toys for the baby before it is born. And when one asks expecting Jewish parents whether they prefer a boy or a girl, their answer is usually, "a healthy child"; they dare not challenge the evil spirits.

Yemenite Jews hang an amulet called a *hamsa* over the crib, trusting that this palm-shaped ornament will prevent Lilith from stealing the newborn. Yemenites and other Sephardim also hide sweets under the baby's bed. To keep the evil spirit busy and away from the newborn, Eastern European Jews traditionally took a harsher, more aggressive approach; they inserted a knife into a Bible, which was then placed under the baby's crib. Garlic was frequently hung in the baby's room.

North African Jews used to greet the birth of a baby boy with greater enthusiasm than the birth of a baby girl. When a baby boy was born in Tunisia (usually at home), a piece of paper covered with blessings and spells against the evil spirits was glued to the door of the mother and baby's room. The father would invite members of his synagogue to *leil shimurim* (a night of prayer that takes place before an important family affair) and serve them cooked broad beans, honey pastries, and liquor. The night before the baby's circumcision, Tunisian Jews burned incense in front of the baby's room while waving a sword to scare Lilith.

There are endless customs and folk traditions surrounding the protection of a newborn baby and his mother. A lot of them probably found their way into Jewish tradition from other cultures. But to those who observe these customs, the origin is not really important, as long as it works.

The birth amulet, above, was used as protection against the evil Lilith. The amulet at right is from Kurdistan and made of welded silver and enamel. Both date from the nineteenth century.

Brit Milah (Circumcision)

The word *brit* in Hebrew means "covenant" and *milah* means "circumcision," for the Bible introduces circumcision as a covenant between God and the people of Israel. Some claim that the act of circumcision stems from real health values, while others connect its origin to blood rituals. Circumcision is not a Jewish invention, and it is not an exclusively Jewish practice. It was, and still is, a puberty rite performed by peoples all over the world. Jews, however, accept circumcision as a divine commandment.

The Jewish faith views *brit milah* as the greatest physical symbol of a baby boy's joining the community of Israel: "Such shall be the covenant between Me and you and your offspring to follow, which you shall keep: Every male among you shall be circumcised. You shall circumcise the flesh of your foreskin, and that shall be the sign of the covenant between Me and you" (Genesis 17:10–11).

12

"Praised be Thou. . . . Who commanded us concerning the rite of circumcision."
This mural from a Prague synagogue depicts a circumcision ceremony.

Decorated with semiprecious stones and mother-of-pearl, this silver filigree circumcision set from Holland dates from the eighteenth century.

Eight days after the birth of a boy (even if it falls on a Sabbath or on Yom Kippur), family and friends gather to celebrate the boy's brit milah, unless the baby is not fit to go through with it. Oftentimes, the newborn is in his room, and the guests take turns peeking at the results of the great miracle of creation. They all await the *mohel*, the specially trained ritual circumciser.

Candles are lit in the room. (In Libya, Jews used to decorate the ceremonial room with red scarves.) A chair is set aside for Elijah the prophet, who is called the angel of the covenant and the children's protector. The baby's father studies all night, watching and protecting his son from all demons (*leil shimurim*), then walks with the baby into the room. (His wife traditionally waits in another room.) "Welcome," say the guests, standing up to honor the infant and his father. They will stand until the end of the ceremony.

Emotions grip the family when the new father then hands the baby over to the mohel, who is dressed in white. He takes the newborn and puts him in the *sandak's* (loosely, godfather's) lap and, before performing his act, recites: "Praised be Thou, O Lord our God, King of the Universe, Who hast sanctified us with Thy command-

*In this eighteenth-century print of a circumcision ceremony, the family gathers
around the baby and his parents to welcome the newborn
Jewish child into the world.*

14

ments and commanded us concerning the rite of circumcision." The foreskin is cut and a drop of blood is spilled. A new boy has entered the Kingdom of Israel: "Praised be Thou, O Lord our God, King of the Universe, Who has sanctified us by Thy commandments, and hast bidden us to make him enter into the covenant of Abraham our father." The guests respond by saying: "As he has been introduced into the covenant, so may he be introduced to the study of the Law, to the nuptial canopy, and to good deeds."

The baby is returned to his mother. Sometimes, the diaper used during the circumcision is made, after it is washed, into a wimple—a piece of cloth that keeps the spools of the Torah together—with both the baby's and parents' names embroidered on it.

As in any Jewish celebration, the guests are then invited to a *seudat mitzvah*, a celebration feast. This feast almost always includes fish, as a sign of fertility, and sweets, as a symbol of the baby's future. God's blessings are invoked on the parents, the sandak, the baby boy, and the mohel, and the coming of the Messiah and of Elijah (herald of the Messiah) is sought.

The **mohel**, *a ritual circumciser, cuts the baby's foreskin, performing the act of circumcision.*

SHMUEL YOSEF AGNON *(1888–1970)*

Considered by many to be the most important Hebrew writer of the twentieth century, S.Y. Agnon wrote fiction about contemporary spiritual concerns as well as the disintegration of traditional ways of life and the loss of faith and identity. His mystic and dreamlike tales were attempts to capture the dying Jewish traditions of old Europe.

Born in Galicia, the son of a follower of the Hasidic Rebbe of Chartkon, Agnon received both a rabbinical and a Hasidic education. In 1907, when he came to Palestine, he was already a well-known Yiddish writer who then made his first steps in Hebrew literature.

Agnon made his home in Jerusalem. He was a very religious Orthodox Jew. His complex personality combined with his great knowledge of the Bible, the Talmud, and Jewish folklore made his literary work compositions of exceptional depth and richness. Agnon symbolizes a peak in modern Hebrew writing. He won the coveted Israel Prize three times and in 1966 was the first Hebrew writer to win the Nobel Prize for Literature.

ROBERT OPPENHEIMER *(1904–1967)*

Born into a wealthy New York family, physicist Robert Oppenheimer attended Harvard University, then went to England. Upon his return to the United States in 1928, he became famous for his research on atomic energy. He was appointed head of the Los Alamos Laboratories in 1943, where the first atom bomb was manufactured. While teaching in various universities, he served as the chairman of the General Advisory Committee to the United States Atomic Energy Commission.

Although he approved the use of the atomic bomb against Japan in World War II, he tried to use his influence to form an international committee to control the use of atomic weapons. Realizing the power of this deadly weapon, he tried fiercely to prevent further research and development in the field of nuclear weaponry. These efforts, as well as some leftist involvement during his youth, brought Senator Joseph McCarthy to persecute him in his anti-Communist campaign, and in 1953, Oppenheimer was suspended by the Atomic Energy Commission as an alleged security risk.

15

If It's a Girl

The birth of a Jewish baby girl is celebrated in a much less emotional atmosphere. The act of circumcision and its symbolism are lacking from any activities surrounding the birth of a girl.

In traditional Jewish families, the birth of a baby girl was celebrated in the synagogue after the birth of the child. The father was called up to the *bimah* (podium) in the synagogue, and a prayer was recited after the reading of the Torah. The act of going up to the bimah for the reading of the Torah is called an *aliyah*. This was also the time when the baby received her name. In today's societies, most girls are named immediately after their birth and the celebration—a feast—takes place either at home or in the synagogue. In Sephardic communities there is a special ceremony called Zebed Habat where parents invite guests to their home and there, during the feast, announce the name they have chosen for their child.

Owing to the growing number of feminist and "New Age" movements within Judaism, new ceremonies have been introduced to celebrate the birth of a girl. Modern communities in Israel celebrate the occasion with a *britah*, a festive meal, to which the parents invite their families and friends. Although most modern ceremonies have no religious base, many incorporate this common blessing from the Zebed Habat ceremony for naming a girl: "May the God Who blessed our fathers Abraham, Isaac, and Jacob, Moses and Aaron, David and Solomon, may He bless the mother and her newborn daughter, whose name in Israel shall be called———. May they raise her for (the study of Torah,) the marriage canopy and for a life of good deeds." Some pray for the newborn Jewish girl to study the Torah and some do not.

Pidyon Haben (Redemption of the Firstborn)

The first issue of the womb of every being, man or beast, that is offered to the Lord shall be yours; but you shall have the firstborn of man redeemed. (Numbers 18:15)

According to tradition, every firstborn male in biblical society dedicated his life to the service of God: "For every firstborn among the Israelites is Mine... I consecrated them to Myself at the time that I smote every firstborn in the land of Egypt" (Numbers 8:17). Primitive tribes in many cases used to sacrifice their firstborn.

After the Israelites worshiped the golden calf, the privilege of serving God was taken away from them and given exclusively to the tribe of Levi. Still, by law, the firstborn belongs to God and therefore must be redeemed.

Although the ceremony was strictly male-oriented and only the father, a Kohen (any man descended from the priestly tribe of *Kohanim*), and the baby boy participated in it, the law of redemption applied and still does apply to the firstborn of the mother by natural birth. If a man married several times, the firstborn of each wife had to be redeemed. If a father never redeems his firstborn for any reason, the boy can do so himself and say the two needed blessings when he comes of age. But the first son of a Kohen or Levite, or whose mother is a daughter of a Kohen or Levite, is exempt from redemption.

You shall have the firstborn of man redeemed. . . . Take as their redemption price, from the age of one month up, the money equivalent of five shekels. (Numbers 18:15–16)

Thirty-one days after the child's birth (except if it falls on a Sabbath or holiday), the baby is placed on a special tray and presented to a Kohen. "This, my firstborn son, is the firstborn of his mother," says the father, "and the Holy one, blessed be He, has given command to redeem him, as it is said, 'And those who are to be redeemed, from a month old shalt thou redeem, according to thine estimation, the money of five shekels. . . .' " (In the United States, the parents now usually use five silver dollars.)

After accepting the redemption money, the Kohen returns the baby to his father and, holding the money over the baby's head, says, "This is instead of that, this is in commutation for that, this is remission of that." Placing his hands on the child's head, he says, "The Lord is thy guardian: The Lord is thy shade upon thy right hand. For length of days, and years of life, and peace shall He add to thee. The Lord shall guard thee from all evil; He shall guard thy soul."

In modern society, redemption of the firstborn functions as a social event that allows the family—sometimes more conveniently than at a brit milah—to gather and celebrate the new addition. Many Jewish communities today let mothers participate in the ceremony by reciting the blessing with the father. And to enhance equality in the community, Reform Jews perform a *pidyon habat*, a redemption of the first daughter.

17

"The first issue of the womb of every being. . . that is offered to the Lord shall be yours; but you shall have the firstborn of man redeemed." This is a Pidyon Haben ceremony (Redemption of the Firstborn) as captured in a 1756 print from Bamberg, Germany.

Weaning Ceremony

And the child grew up, and was weaned, and Abraham held a great feast on the day that Isaac was weaned. (Genesis 21:8)

Weaning ceremonies are traditional, although no biblical law requires a Jew to celebrate the weaning of his child. Jews have performed weaning ceremonies in various personal ways: family gatherings, feasts, prayers, and songs. The weaning ceremony is a celebration of the changing relationship between a mother and her child, one more step in her offspring's path of life.

It is a vanishing custom now, but there are numerous stories of mothers breast-feeding their children up to a late age. One famous true story tells of a young Jewish boy in the small village of Szebzeshin, Poland, who was breast-fed until the age of five. His weaning ceremony included all his preschool friends and relatives, who didn't see anything wrong with the custom. One wonders, today, if an American boy would tolerate such a public ceremony.

Some young Jewish communities are trying to reintroduce weaning ceremonies into Jewish life, feeling it can give the problem-stricken modern family an opportunity to meet, celebrate, and bond.

JONAS EDWARD SALK (1914–)

Jonas Salk, a physician and medical researcher, became world famous in 1953 when he developed the polio vaccine.

Born in New York City, Salk showed distinction as a researcher at a young age and became a consultant in epidemic diseases to the United States Secretary of the Army. In 1949, he was appointed Professor of Bacteriology and Head of the Department of Preventive Medicine at the University of Pittsburgh. He was made a Fellow of the American Public Health Association and the American Association for the Advancement of Science.

ELIEZER BEN YEHUDA (1858–1922)

Eliezer Ben Yehuda was the father of modern Hebrew and one of the first active Zionist leaders. Born in Lithuania, he was sent at the age of five to a Hasidic yeshiva, where he was secretly introduced to secular literature. He then went to Paris to study medicine, and there became enthusiastic about Zionism and about the revival of the ancient Hebrew language. In Paris, he published articles about the need for Jews to work for the national revival of their homeland.

When he fell ill with tuberculosis, Ben Yehuda decided to quit his medical studies and move to the better climate of Palestine. He enrolled in the Alliance Seminary to enable himself to teach at the agricultural school of Mikveh Israel in Palestine. After meeting the Jerusalem scholar A.M. Luntz, who was a Hebrew speaker, he was finally convinced that Jews could not be unified unless their children revived Hebrew as their spoken language.

After arriving in Jaffa in 1881, he informed his wife that from that day on they would speak only Hebrew. The Ben Yehuda family became the first Hebrew-speaking household in Palestine.

Ben Yehuda wrote numerous articles that appeared in newspapers all over the country. He took a teacher's position at the Jerusalem Alliance school on the condition that he would be permitted to teach in Hebrew, thus creating the first Hebrew-language school.

After his wife's death in 1891, Ben Yehuda married her sister, who adopted the Hebrew name of Hemdah and joined forces with him in campaigning for Hebrew-language usage. Ben Yehuda and his family spoke vigorously against traditional Judaism; as a result, the Orthodox community informed the Turkish authorities about this rebellious Jew, who was then sentenced to one year in prison. He appealed and was released.

Ben Yehuda is the creator of the simple, popular style of modern Hebrew and was the first person to make a regular systematic practice of coining common Hebrew words. He was also the first to create a Hebrew dictionary, which served as a base for the modern Hebrew dictionaries.

BAR/BAT MITZVAH

"Blessed is He Who has freed me from responsibility for this child's conduct," say fathers thirteen years after the birth of their son. Thirteen years after joining the community of Israel by circumcision, a boy takes yet another step on the path of Jewish life: to become a *bar mitzvah*, a son of the commandment. Twelve (or, in some communities, thirteen) years after birth, a girl enters her world of adulthood by way of a *bat mitzvah*. From then on the youngsters assume all the responsibilities of adult Jews.

There is no single answer to the question of why this significant point in life, this celebration of puberty, occurs at the age of thirteen for boys and twelve for girls. It is clear, however, that the tradition is about two thousand years old. Although it is the most universally celebrated event in Jewish life, the bar mitzvah is never mentioned in the Bible. Celebrations of the bar mitzvah began during the Middle Ages, when it took on a similar form to the one we know today. The bat mitzvah began in the 1920s.

As his father looks on, the bar mitzvah boy reads his portion of the Torah, taking on his responsibilities in the community as an adult.

20

Beginning the day of his bar mitzvah, a boy will wear tefillin every day during morning prayers, except on the Sabbath and holidays.

Preparation begins several months, sometimes a year or more, before the boy's thirteenth birthday. He must prepare for the day when he will be called in front of the congregation to chant from the *haftarah* (selection from the Prophets) that accompanies the Torah reading for that day, and sometimes (especially in more traditional congregations) from the Torah reading itself. With a special teacher, the young boy learns to properly sing (according to special biblical notes called *ta'amei hamikrah*) his haftarah or Torah passages. From this birthday on, he will be a full-fledged Jewish man; he must observe all of the commandments. After this birthday, a young man can be counted as part of a *minyan*, a quorum of ten adult males.

Bar or bat mitzvah is another emotional stage in Jewish rites of passage. Different contexts gave birth to different customs for celebrating a bar or bat mitzvah, but the basic structure and ceremonies are the same. The celebration itself usually takes place on a Sabbath, although it can take place on any day the Torah is read—Monday, Thursday, or the first day of a new month.

The bar mitzvah boy completes his recitation of his Torah and haftarah passages, and with the accompanying blessings, the young man is now expected to give a speech, or *derasha*, prepared by him and his teacher. He offers an interpretation (usually traditional and homiletic) of his Torah or haftarah portion; thanks all the people who have helped him along during his first thirteen years—parents, grandparents, friends, relatives, and teachers—and invites the members of the community to *kiddush* (the blessing over wine) and a small feast.

Today, most Jewish families celebrate their son's bar mitzvah with a reception after the ceremony, which often takes place outside the synagogue. In recent years, these parties have often reached extravagant peaks, with each family trying to outdo the other. Food, entertainers, and musicians are hired; the more people invited, the better. Yet the meaningful tradition can be overwhelmed by an exaggerated celebration that removes the bar mitzvah from its true origins and makes people forget the ideas behind the ritual.

Often, when watching modern celebrations one yearns for the modest intimacy of the past. North African Jewish communities used to celebrate a bar mitzvah only on Mondays or Thursdays. On the eve of the celebration, they would cut the boy's hair before guests came to dinner. On the following day, the boy's friends led him to the synagogue, where he put on *tefillin* (phylacteries) for the first time and was then called to the Torah to recite. Family members gave out fragrance bottles, exchanged gifts, and later, at home, served first a light meal and then a sit-down dinner.

In most Jewish communities when a boy turns thirteen he begins to wear a *tallit*, or prayer shawl, in synagogue. The tallit is rectangular and has four fringes that represent the four corners of the universe God created. When counted together, the knots of the fringes and the four fringes themselves add up to 613, the number of commandments in the Torah.

The Torah does not state, however, when a person should start wearing a tallit, so various groups introduce it into their children's lives at different ages. Among Sephardic Jews in Israel, it is custom to give a boy his tallit when he is five or six years old. Many Ashkenazic Jews would traditionally not wear a tallit until they were married. (A wife would often give her groom a tallit as a wedding gift.) Some Orthodox Jews still follow that tradition, but most Conservative Jews present a tallit to the boy at his bar mitzvah.

On the occasion of his bar mitzvah, a boy also begins to put on tefillin, in fulfillment of the commandment, "And thou shall bind (these words [of the Torah]) for a sign upon thine hand, and they shall be for frontlets between thine eyes." Tefillin consist of two square black boxes attached to long leather straps. The boxes contain prescribed verses from the Torah, written on strips of parchment. The bar mitzvah boy is supposed to wear the tefillin during morning prayers every

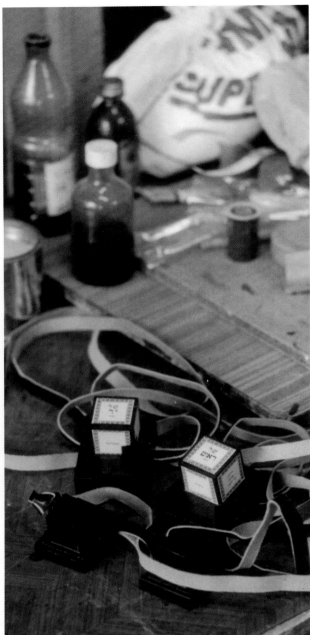

In most Jewish communities, when a boy turns thirteen he begins to wear a tallit, a prayer shawl (left), and also begins to put on the tefillin (right).

day, except on the Sabbath and holidays. In some Jewish communities, a boy begins wearing tefillin a month before his thirteenth birthday, in others beginning a day after, and in still others a year before his bar mitzvah.

Following Israel's victory in the Six Day War and the reunification of Jerusalem, a new tradition developed among some American Jews—to celebrate a bar mitzvah by the Western Wall, which symbolizes the tie between the boy, his God, and his land.

The bat mitzvah is an invention of the twentieth century. It is celebrated with a festive meal, and as in a bar mitzvah observance, the girl delivers a speech, or derasha, and reads the Torah or haftarah portion. Some bat mitzvah ceremonies, however, are held in the synagogue on Friday evening rather than Saturday morning.

*Tefillin consist of two square black boxes attached to long
leather straps. The boxes contain prescribed verses
from the Torah.*

23

Modern Reform and Conservative communities in the United States celebrate the bat mitzvah in the same manner as they celebrate the bar mitzvah: the girl gets an aliyah, often wears a tallit, and sometimes even puts on tefillin. These practices have created much controversy in the Jewish world, for Orthodox Judaism forbids a woman from taking part in such activities. In Israel, a bat mitzvah is only a social event and does not have, in most cases, any religious significance.

MARRIAGE

"And the Lord God said: 'It is not good that man should be alone'" (Genesis 2:18). From this verse came the understanding that marriage is a central duty of Jewish life. Traditionally, Jewish men and women are not considered whole until they find their mates.

Engagement

Prior to the twentieth century, Jewish girls rarely left the house, and their fathers arranged their marriages, sometimes even before their birth. Jews in nineteenth-century Eastern Europe considered a scholar to be an appropriate groom. No need to be rich, they thought, as long as one studied the Torah. A good bride had to be beautiful *and* wealthy. For women, beauty was a matter of geography. In Eastern Europe, it meant having beautiful eyes. Moroccan women needed to have a double chin, be chubby, and have a dimple in order to be considered beautiful; a skinny Moroccan bride might be likened by her mother-in-law to "a candle holder wearing a skirt."

Although the Talmud says that all matches are made in heaven, most parents didn't leave it to heaven and instead hired the services of a matchmaker, a *shadchan*. This colorful institution flourished in most Eastern European communities and gave rise to a rich folklore. One tale tells of a Jewish matchmaker who took a young man to visit a prospective bride. When they left, the matchmaker said, "Didn't I tell you? What a great family! And so wealthy! Did you see the beautiful silverware on the table?" "Maybe," said the young man, "they borrowed it to impress me." "Nonsense," said the matchmaker, "who would lend those thieves anything?"

24

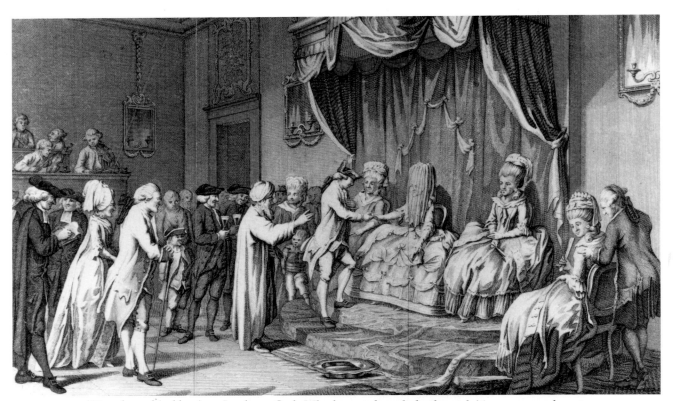

"You abound in blessing, Lord our God, Who has made us holy through Your commandments and has commanded us concerning marriage. . ." This print captures a marriage ceremony of Portuguese Jews.

JOSEPH PULITZER *(1847–1911)*

Joseph Pulitzer, a Hungarian Jew who immigrated to the United States, became a well-known name in the world of journalism and literature. A lawyer by profession, he bought the *New York World*, which became one of the leading newspapers in the country.

A philanthropist and political activist, Pulitzer served in the Union Army during the Civil War and was a member of the United States House of Representatives. He donated the money necessary for the establishment of the acclaimed School of Journalism at Columbia University in New York City.

In his will, Pulitzer left money for various scholarships, but his most notable achievement was the establishment of the Pulitzer Prizes, which have become the most prestigious literary and journalistic awards in the United States and have been awarded each May since 1917.

As shown in this wedding scene taken from the Sefer Minhagim *(the Book of Customs, Amsterdam, 1662), the wedding couple is married under the* chupa *(canopy).*

25

Until the twentieth century, most Jewish marriages in Eastern Europe and in North Africa were arranged either by matchmakers or by parents. As soon as both sets of parents agreed on a match, decided on the financial arrangements, and fixed a date for the wedding, the couple became engaged. The two families then met, and the groom gave the bride's parents gifts. In strict Orthodox families, this was the only time the bride was allowed to meet her husband prior to the wedding; this custom dates back thousands of years and is still in practice in some Hasidic circles. Matchmaking and dating services exist in more modern formats—including computerized services—to this day, serving communities that would like to shield their members from interfaith marriages.

The Wedding

In biblical times, the groom's father paid the bride's family a dowry for the privilege of marrying her. Many young boys who couldn't afford to pay for their desired woman married late. This problem was solved by the marriage contract, or *ketubah*, which exists to this day. The groom's family did not have to worry anymore about a dowry as the groom promised, in writing, to pay the bride whatever they agreed upon, in case of divorce or death.

"Behold, you are consecrated to me with this ring according to the law of Moses and Israel." These two wedding rings (left) are from the collection of the Jewish Museum in New York City.

A ketubah (right) is a marriage contract whereby the groom promises to pay the bride a previously agreed upon dowry in case of divorce or death. This is a Tunisian ketubah from 1858.

26

On the Sabbath before the wedding day, the bride and groom and their families went to synagogue, where the groom was honored with an aliyah. After the blessings, the community threw candies at the couple to wish them a sweet life. This ritual is still practiced in many Jewish communities, including Israel.

Jews in ancient times were married in autumn, after the harvest. Friday was the most popular day for weddings; the ceremony took place in the morning and the feast then became part of the Sabbath dinner, thus saving on expenses. Tuesday was also popular because when God created the world that was the day he said twice, "It is good." In many cultures, Tuesday is still a very popular day for weddings. A couple cannot get married, however, on a Sabbath or major holiday or on certain other days in the Jewish year.

Weddings were traditionally celebrated at the groom's house. Both the bride and the groom fasted on their wedding day. The bride first bathed, perfumed, and dressed in a white gown with her finest jewelry. The groom wore a white robe. Treated like king and queen on their wedding day, both wore olive-leaf crowns. Once ready, the bride was carried on a special chair into the groom's house; this welcomed the bride into her new home.

The ceremony itself took place under the open sky, with all the guests wishing the young couple to have as many children as the stars. Originally a Jewish wedding consisted of two stages: *erusin*, in which the woman is betrothed, and *nissuin*, in which the actual union is consecrated through seven blessings. In ancient times, these two stages took place as much as a year apart. Today, the two rites are combined.

NELLY SACHS *(1891–1970)*

Nobel Prize winner Nelly Sachs was the daughter of a Berlin industrialist who encouraged the arts in his home. At the age of seventeen, she began writing neo-Romantic poetry in traditional rhymed forms and plays with a fairy tale flavor.

Her first works reflected a Christian intellectual world filled with mysticism. Like many assimilated Jews, Sachs discovered her Jewish heritage only around 1933, when anti-Semitism grew in Europe.

Nelly Sachs' reputation is based largely on the material she wrote during World War II and published soon after; this work describes her own experiences and the sufferings of the European Jews. In 1940, she immigrated to Sweden. The motif of flight and pursuit, the symbol of the hunter and his quarry, are at the core of her poetic thought. Although she wrote in free verse, Sachs' writing combines craftsmanship with exquisite language, and is filled with mysterious atmosphere. In 1966, she shared the Nobel Prize in literature with S.Y. Agnon.

Some ancient customs have now vanished from the wedding ceremony, but many still remain, although in slightly different form. The bride and groom stay in separate rooms before the wedding. The groom and his friends sit with the rabbi and review the ketubah. The rabbi then asks the groom whether he agrees to the terms of the marriage contract. Two witnesses must hear his answer; then they sign the ketubah. In less traditional ceremonies, the ketubah serves more as a memento of tradition and less as an actual contract.

Now all is ready for the big moment. Guests may hold lit candles. The groom walks up to the bride, who is now sitting on a thronelike chair. He looks at her, then covers her face with a veil. The fathers of both bride and groom escort the groom to the *chupa*, the wedding canopy. The mothers of the bride and groom then escort the bride—or sometimes the respective sets of parents escort the groom and (then) the bride.

Originally the chupa was a tallit stretched across the top of four poles cut from trees that were planted when the wedding couple was born. Four close friends or relatives each held one of the poles. Today most weddings take place under an embroidered canopy, which is held up by store-bought poles.

The bride sometimes circles the groom seven (or three) times—sometimes accompanied by her mother and mother-in-law to be. Taking a cup of wine, the rabbi says: "You abound in blessings, Lord our God, Who has made us holy through Your commandments and has commanded us concerning marriages that are forbidden and those that are permitted when carried out under the canopy and with the sacred wedding ceremonies. You abound in blessings, Lord our God, Who makes Your people of Israel holy through this rite of the canopy and the sacred bond of marriage."

The groom then puts an unbroken gold ring on the bride's index finger and says: "Behold, you are consecrated to me with this ring according to the law of Moses and Israel." The rabbi (or another person) reads the ketubah out loud and gives it to the bride to keep. He or others read the traditional seven blessings and the bride and groom drink wine from the same cup, which symbolizes the beginning of their life together. The ceremony ends dramatically when the groom breaks a glass wrapped in a handkerchief, a reminder, perhaps, of the destruction of the Temple. The guests say, "Mazal tov!" After the ceremony, in more religious communities the newlyweds go off to consummate the marriage (*yichud*); this is the first time they will have been together alone. When they return, they are officially considered husband and wife. In most communities, however, a reception follows the ceremony and a symbolic period of yichud (if any).

In North Africa, both the bride's and groom's hands are covered with henna, a symbol of fertile life, in a prewedding ceremony.

JAN PEERCE *(1904–1984)*

Born in New York as Jacob Pincus Perelmuth, Jan Peerce launched his musical career as a dance band violinist and singer while studying medicine. In 1933, he signed up for a long-term engagement at Radio City Music Hall in New York. It was there that the legendary conductor Arturo Toscanini heard him sing. He invited Peerce to sing with the NBC Symphony Orchestra in 1938. After his operatic debut in 1941 in Philadelphia and a recital in New York, he was cast to sing the lead in *La Traviata* at New York's Metropolitan Opera House. His colorful voice, along with his distinctive interpretation of both Italian and German operas, made him one of opera's great tenors. Peerce did not neglect his Jewish background, however; he appeared in cantorial recitals and recorded cantorial works.

30

Weddings have always been great occasions for large celebrations. In Eastern Europe, those who could afford it gave a grand feast. Klezmer musicians entertained the guests and a special comedian, or *badchan*, was hired. The celebration usually lasted until the early morning hours.

In the old North African Jewish communities, wedding ceremonies lasted eight days and nights. In Tunisia, a week before the wedding the groom sent his bride a satin basket that contained his wedding gifts: perfume, shoes, jewelry, dried fruits, and two large candles, which would be lit under the canopy.

Yemenite and some North African Jews still conduct a prewedding henna ceremony. The bride is dressed in a luxurious dress and fine jewelry. A special crown rests on top of her head. Candles wrapped with basil leaves are lit, and the beat of metal boxes used as drums echoes throughout the house. The bride's mother walks in with a candlelit plate containing red henna (a dye sometimes used to color hair). The mother covers the bride's and groom's hands with henna, wishing them a long, fertile life. Afterward, food is served.

One custom that used to take place among the Yemenites was a wedding game. On the Sabbath before the wedding, the groom and his friends were invited to the bride's house for a game of "finding the chicken." The groom would search the house for a stuffed chicken. When he found it, everyone would cheer and eat the stuffed bird.

In Tunisia in the past, the wedding blessings were recited by the rabbi in the synagogue. Tunisian rabbis did not read the ketubah. The meal at the wedding was usually light, but each guest received a piece of cake to take home. The bride also prepared little bags of fine cloth filled with sweets for her single girlfriends.

It used to be that in Libya, seven days before the wedding a group of boys would escort the groom wherever he went, and a group of girls would do the same for the bride. They would visit friends and relatives and take part in festive meals. On Wednesday, the day before the wedding (all weddings in Libya took place on Thursdays), the bride was accompanied to the groom's house with songs and cheers. The groom went up to the roof and threw a jar of water into the backyard of the house. The jar would break and the water would spill. The bride then walked on the spilled water while the women sang: "Oh, you groom, break the jar..." This ancient, moving, and almost sexual ritual symbolized the unity of the newlyweds. Also in Libya, the Jews did not use a canopy held by people. Instead the groom covered himself and his bride with a tallit, a metaphorical symbol of the protection he offered and God provided her. They remained covered until the rabbi completed his recital of the seven blessings.

SIGMUND FREUD *(1856–1939)*

Sigmund Freud, the father of psychoanalysis, was born in Germany and studied in Vienna, where he spent most of his life. Early on in his career, Freud became interested in hypnosis as a form of treatment for hysteria cases. He claimed that the repression of emotions in the unconscious could produce symptoms of hysteric illness. From this grew his technique of "free association," out of which his theory of psychoanalysis evolved.

Freud's theory was designed to explain the motives of people's deeds as a way of helping the mentally ill. He went on to analyze people's sexual lives, believing that sex played an important role in the cause of neurosis. In order to prove his theory, he began analyzing himself in 1897 and discovered that dream analysis could help psychiatric treatment. Although he encountered tremendous opposition, Freud's success in treating patients brought him great admiration and a large following. But only after he escaped the Nazis and moved to London did the world recognize his genius. His theory has had wide impact; his methods survive today and are profoundly influential in modern psychotherapy and psychiatry.

Moroccan Jews usually celebrated their lavish weddings on Wednesdays. They placed the canopy—beautifully decorated with colorful fabrics and boasting a large crown on top—on a platform. Singers and poets recited songs for entertainment. A day after the ceremony, the guests greeted the newlyweds with sweet doughnuts, honey, and milk. These ceremonies lasted for seven days.

Marriage and Sexuality

Sexuality is perceived in Judaism as a positive activity. Jewish sources describe sex as holy and good. It is a legitimate *mitzvah*, a positive commandment. Ideally, marriage protects the partners from trivializing their relationship.

Jewish religious marriages are governed by the biblical precept of: "You shall not come near a woman while she is impure by her uncleanness to uncover her nakedness" (Leviticus, 18:19). According to tradition and the laws of *niddah*, an Ashkenazi husband was prohibited from all sexual contact with his wife for five full days starting from the beginning of the wife's monthly menstrual period (for Sephardim, it was six days). The Talmud extended that date by seven days after the end of the menstrual period, therefore making the period of separation last an average of twelve days (thirteen for Sephardim). During that time, the husband and wife could not sleep in the same bed.

After the period of "uncleanness," the woman bathed and then purified herself spiritually in the *mikveh* (ritual bath). After she completely immersed herself in the water in an upright position, she recited, "Blessed art Thou, Lord our God, King of the universe, who has sanctified us with His commandments and commanded us concerning the immersion."

According to biblical law, a woman was also considered impure for forty days after giving birth to a boy, and eighty days after delivering a girl. Purity laws are still kept, but only in the most religious Jewish families. To a modern person, such laws might seem ancient and primitive, but a deeper interpretation reveals a more practical side. People who practice the purity laws believe that they help sexual relationships by avoiding routine and maintaining high levels of desire in both husband and wife.

31

Divorce

Almost no divorces occurred in ancient times. Modern Judaism, however, recognizes the possibility of terminating a marriage. After visiting a civil court, a couple seeking to divorce must go to the rabbi to ask for a bill of divorcement, a *get*. Two witnesses and a scribe, a *sofer*, must be present at the time. The rabbi first tries to reconcile the two parties. If they decide to go ahead with the divorce, the husband and wife are sent into two separate rooms to wait for the scribe to write out the get.

When the scribe is finished writing the bill of divorcement, the rabbi calls the couple into the room. He asks the wife whether she accepts the divorce. If she does, the husband releases her from their marriage. Both the rabbi and the

During a get *(divorce) ceremony, the wife stretches out her arms, while her husband places the* get *(divorce document) in her hands.*

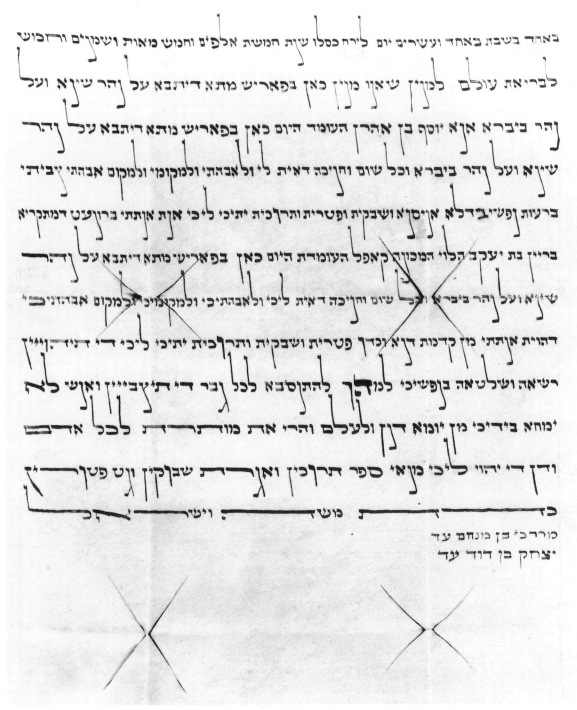

באחד בשבת באחד ועשרין יום ליח כסלו שית חמשת אלפים וחנוש מאות ושמנים ורחמש

לבריאת עולם למנין שאנו מנין כאן בפאריש מתא דיתבא על נהר שינא ועל

נהר ביברא אנא יוסף בן אהרן העומד היום כאן בפאריש מתא דיתבא על נהר

שינא ועל נהר ביברא וכל שום וחניכה דאית לי ולאבהתי ולמקומי ולמקום אבהתי צביתי

ברעות וצביב דלא אניסא ושבקית ופטרית ותרכית יתיכי ליכי אנת אנתתי ברוועט דמתקריא

בריין בת יעקב הלוי המכונה קאפל העומדת היום כאן בפאריש מתא דיתבא על דהר

שינא ועל נהר ביברא וכל שום וחניכה דאית לי ולאבהתיכי ולמקומניכי ולמקום אבהתניכי

דהוית אנתתי מן קדמת דנא וכדן פטרית ושבקית ותרכית יתיכי ליכי די דנידיין

רשאה ושלטאה בנפשיכי למהך להתנסבא לכל גבר די תיצביין ואנש לא

ימחא בידיכי מן יומא דין ולעלם והרי את מותרת ליכי לכל אדם

ודן די יהוי ליכי מנאי ספר תרוכין ואגרת שבוקין וגט פטורין

כדת משה וישראל

מרדכי בן מנחם עד

יצחק בן דוד עד

There is much formality involved in granting a bill of divorce. This divorce document, a get, *is from Paris and dates back to 1824. After the ceremony, the* get *was cut so that it could not be reused.*

witnesses sign the paper. The husband then hands the get to his wife. She stretches out her arms, holds her palms close to each other, and he places the get in her hands. She then closes her hands, puts the get under her arm, and walks out of the room. When she returns, the witnesses reiterate to the rabbi that the document is indeed the document they signed. The scribe also confirms that this is the correct document, and the husband confirms that he really asked the scribe to write it. The rabbi then folds the document and cuts its corners, making sure that it can't be used again. As in marriage, so in divorce: the woman keeps the document.

DEATH

According to Jewish tradition, God gives each person a soul before birth, and it is returned to God once the person's life has ended. This world, *olam hazeh*, is only a preparation for the world to come, *olam habah*. A person's suffering in this world will be compensated in the world to come.

Judaism encourages mourning over the death of a close relative but only to a certain extent, so that the mourning will not be interpreted as doubting God's order. The Jewish attitude toward death is summed up in this quote from Job: "The Lord gave, and the Lord hath taken away: Blessed be the name of the Lord" (Job 1:21).

Members of a grieving family close the eyes of a deceased and cover his face with a sheet. A candle is lit in the house. All mirrors are covered, honoring the dead person who can no longer see himself and preventing the mourners from looking at themselves and thus forgetting their grief. The chief mourners, *avelim*, for the deceased are the mother, father, son, daughter, brother, sister, and spouse. Before the funeral these mourners make a small tear in their clothing near their heart, as a public announcement of grief.

Because embalming is forbidden, Jews leave the body in its natural state. The burial, therefore, must be done quickly, usually within twenty-four hours. The body is washed, just as it was washed at birth, and clothed in linen shrouds. It is then wrapped in a simple cloth with no pockets, showing that the person's value was not in the contents of his pockets but in his spirit. The deceased's tallit is buried with him, with one fringe cut. In the United States, a simple wooden coffin containing the soil of Israel serves for burial; in Israel people are usually buried in a bed of reeds. A small opening is left in all coffins to let the body touch the earth, honoring the Torah's saying: "For dust you are and to dust shall you return" (Genesis 3:19).

34

In the United States, a simple wooden coffin serves for burial. This sarcophagus from Italy, however, is much more elaborate.

The mourners circling the coffin in this 1723 print by Picart are Sephardic Jews from Amsterdam.

35

Friends and relatives stand in front of the covered body to recite a special mourning prayer (*eil malei rachamim*), after which they carry the deceased's body to the burial site, where they stand in front of the open grave. Carrying the body is considered a great honor to the deceased: he can never repay you for this kindness. At the graveside, the mourners recite a *kaddish*, the mourning prayer, which according to law and custom, will also be recited every day for eleven months for one's parents and then on each anniversary of the death:

> *Magnified and sanctified be His great name in the world which He created according to His will. May He establish His kingdom during your life and during your days, and during the life of all the house of Israel, speedily and in the near future, and say, Amen. May His great name be blessed forever and ever. Blessed, praised and glorified, exalted and honored, adored and lauded be the Name of the Holy One, Blessed be He Who is beyond all blessings and hymns, praises and songs that are uttered in the world; and say, Amen. May there be abundant peace from heaven, and life for us and for all Israel; and say Amen. May He who maketh peace in the heavens, make peace for us and for all Israel; and say, Amen.*

Then, those at the cemetery throw a handful of earth on the coffin after it has been lowered into the ground. After the funeral, the mourners return to the bereaved's home, where family and friends serve a meal of consolation, a *seudat havra'ah*. The mourners light a special candle that will stay lit for seven days, the

36

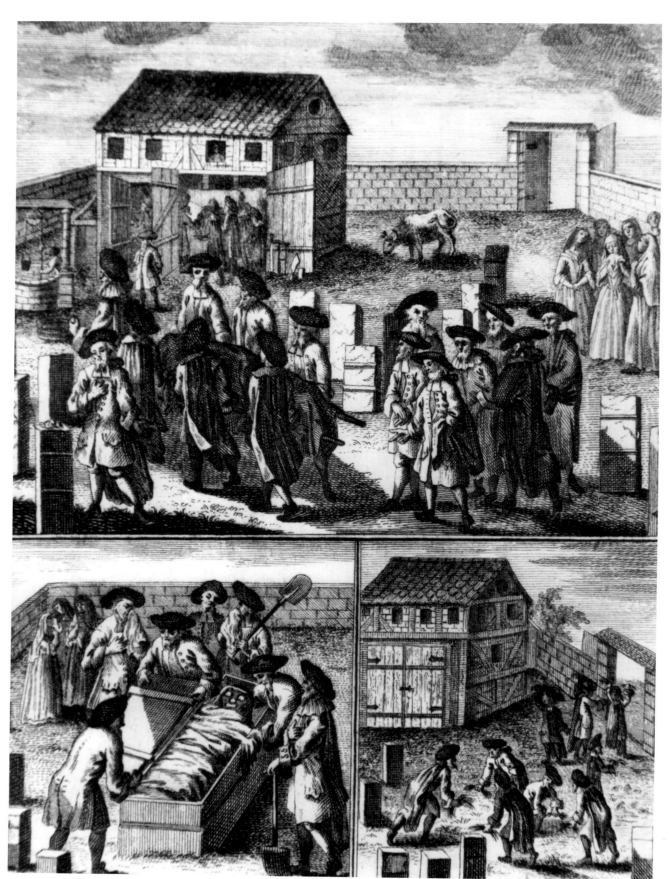

Jews leave the body in its natural state. The burial, therefore, must be done quickly, usually within twenty-four hours. Those at the cemetery throw a handful of earth on the coffin after it has been lowered into the ground.

Carrying the body is considered a great honor to the deceased. This print captures a burial scene in Venice.

days they are required to remain at home to mourn, or "sit *shivah.*" During this time, the mourners wear dark clothes; some do not change out of the torn clothing they wore to the funeral. They do not wash or shave and do not leave the house. People in some houses still keep the tradition of sitting on the floor during shivah. A minyan gathers or is arranged by the synagogue, and the ten (or more) men recite the kaddish every morning and evening. The mourners may then eat, but they are not allowed to cook during shivah, so friends and relatives bring them food.

After the seven days have passed, the mourners return to work and try to resume normal life. For thirty days, they are not allowed to attend social events or celebrations; parents avoid all celebrations for a full year. The mourners continue to say kaddish for eleven months. In some cases, a tombstone will be set on the grave on the thirtieth day after the burial (*shloshim*), and in some cases, it will be erected after a year's time in a short unveiling ceremony. Every year, on the date of death, the family lights a candle in the house, visits the grave for a memorial ceremony, and recites the kaddish.

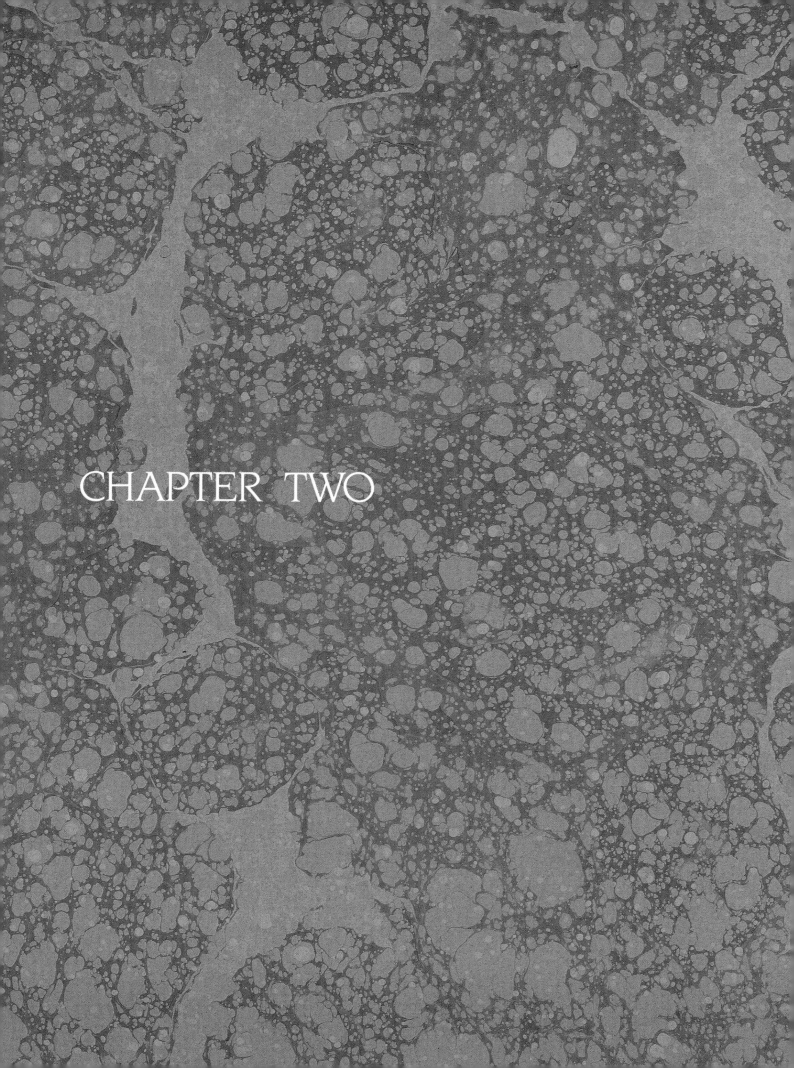

CHAPTER TWO

LIVING THE TRADITION

Although their numbers are comparatively few, Jews invariably attract world attention. Their beliefs and unique way of life continue to inspire their fellow man. Jewish ritual and behavior serve as models for many others around the world.

Jews in different countries evolved different traditions. In the tenth century, a new term sprang up—"Ashkenazim"—to refer to those Jews who lived in Germany and northern France. In later years, Eastern European and Scandinavian Jews also became known as Ashkenazim. Most Ashkenazic Jews spoke Yiddish, which dates back to the tenth or eleventh century. Jews who lived in Spain or other Mediterranean countries were called "Sephardim." Sephardic Jews fled Spain and Portugal at the end of the fifteenth century and found refuge in the Turkish Empire, Greece, and Bulgaria (where they preserved their own dialect called Ladino), as well as Syria, Palestine, North Africa, Italy, Holland, and South America.

Ashkenazim and Sephardim differ in culture, social customs, and ritual. Despite these differences, Sephardic and Ashkenazic Jews are one people who share through Judaism great bonds with their God, their land, and their Torah.

The Torah

Seven weeks after their exodus from Egypt, the children of Israel witnessed what became the essence of Judaism: God's giving of the Ten Commandments to Moses. Through Moses, God gave the Tribes of Israel His written code of ethics and religion. The acceptance of these Ten Commandments, of the entire Torah, and of God's subsequent revelations to the Prophets of Israel is the core of Judaism:

40

I am the Lord thy God, who brought thee out of the Land of Egypt, out of the house of bondage;
Thou shalt have no other gods before Me;
Thou shalt not take the name of the Lord thy God in vain;
Remember the Sabbath day to keep it holy;
Honor thy father and thy mother;
Thou shalt not murder;
Thou shalt not commit adultery;
Thou shalt not steal;
Thou shalt not bear false witness against thy neighbor;
Thou shalt not covet anything that belongs to thy neighbor.

For forty years, God spoke to Moses through divine prophecy; God's words were captured and written in the Torah, the Five Books of Moses. These five books form the basis of Jewish life. God spoke directly to Moses, who repeated the words to the leaders of Israel, and these leaders then related them to their disciples. In the first five centuries of the common era, the "oral Torah" was recorded in the Talmud. The Talmud consists of the Mishna, the first Jewish code of laws after the Bible, and the Gemara, an elaboration of the Mishna. The laws governing religious and civil practice in every phase of Jewish life are collectively called the *halachah*. The Hebrew Bible consists also of the Prophets (*Nevi'im*) and the Sacred Writings (*Ketuvim*), which includes the Psalms, the Song of Songs, and the books of Esther, Job, and Ecclesiastes, among others.

God's words were written down in the Torah, the Five Books of Moses.

Marc Chagall's painting King David *can be found in Israel's Knesset.*

42

45

In the synagogue, the scrolls of the Torah are kept in the Torah ark (left).
This seventeenth-century door (above) for a Torah ark is from Cracow, Poland.

46

*The Torah ark is covered with curtains that are beautifully
embroidered with symbols and scenes from Jewish life.*

This Torah crown from Venice (above, left), which dates back to 1752, is used as an ornament to beautify a Torah scroll.

Decorated with Jewish and Hebrew symbols, this ornament (above) is placed on the Torah scrolls.

These two pointers (left), which are put on top of the Torah scrolls, are from Italy.

This page from the Mishne Torah, *a book by Moses Maimonides, dates back to 1180.*

אִישׁ אֶחָד מִן הָרָמָתַ
הָרְמָתַיִם צוֹפִים מֵהַר
אֶפְרַיִם וּשְׁמוֹ אֶלְקָנָה
בֶּן יְרֹחָם בֶּן אֱלִיהוּא
בֶּן תֹּחוּ בֶן צוּף אֶפְרָתִי
וְלוֹ שְׁתֵּי נָשִׁים שֵׁם
אַחַת חַנָּה וְשֵׁם הַשֵּׁנִית
פְּנִנָּה וַיְהִי לִפְנִנָּה
יְלָדִים וּלְחַנָּה אֵין יְלָ
דִים וְעָלָה הָאִישׁ ז

הַהוּא מֵעִירוֹ מִיָּמִים
יָמִימָה לְהִשְׁתַּחֲוֹת
וְלִזְבֹּחַ לַיהוָה צְבָאוֹת
בְּשִׁלֹה וְשָׁם שְׁנֵי בְנֵ
עֵלִי חָפְנִי וּפִנְחָס כֹּה
נִים לַיהוָה וַיְהִי
הַיּוֹם וַיִּזְבַּח אֶלְקָנָה ז
וְנָתַן לִפְנִנָּה אִשְׁתּוֹ
וּלְכָל בָּנֶיהָ וּבְנוֹתֶיהָ ז
מָנוֹת וּלְחַנָּה יִתֵּן מָנָה

אַחַת אַפַּיִם כִּי אֶת חַנָּה
אָהֵב וַיהוָה סָגַר רַחְמ
רַחְמָהּ וְכִעֲסַתָּה צָרָ
צָרָתָהּ גַּם כַּעַס בַּעֲבוּר
הַרְּעִמָהּ כִּי סָגַר יְהוָה
בְּעַד רַחְמָהּ וְכֵן יַעֲשֶׂה
שָׁנָה בְשָׁנָה מִדֵּי עֲלֹ
עֲלֹתָהּ בְּבֵית יְהוָה
כֵּן תַּכְעִסֶנָּה וַתִּבְכֶּה
וְלֹא תֹאכַל וַיֹּאמֶר ז

This is a page from a fourteenth-century German Bible.

AMADEO MODIGLIANI *(1884–1920)*

Amadeo Modigliani studied painting in his native country of Italy until 1906, when he went to Paris. He began exhibiting in 1915 after coming under the influence of Cezanne, the Cubists, and medieval art.

A brilliant and highly individual painter, Modigliani evolved a highly personal style. He became famous for his portraits and nudes of "long" women, but not until after he died at thirty-six from excessive use of drugs and alcohol. He is now considered among the greatest of modern artists.

OSCAR HAMMERSTEIN II *(1895–1960)*

Oscar Hammerstein II is remembered as the person who gave the musical play its integrated dramatic form. The prestigious Broadway musical owes its status and achievement as an artistic form to Hammerstein, who started his career in New York as a stage manager working for his uncle.

His first independent job was writing and producing the book for three Broadway musicals. His major success stories in the Broadway of the twen-

ties were *Rose Marie, The Desert Song*, and *Show Boat*.

Hammerstein went on to Hollywood for a few years, but returned to form his legendary partnership with Richard Rodgers. Together they wrote and produced musicals with a style all their own. Over the years, they created such classic hits as *Oklahoma, Carousel, South Pacific* (which won a Pulitzer Prize), *The King and I*, and *The Sound of Music*. Their contribution to the world is perpetuated by the Rodgers and Hammerstein Foundation in New York, which supplies funds for various philanthropic causes.

Dietary Laws (*Kashrut*)

An old Hasidic legend tells of Rabbi Jehuda, who asked the head of a Jewish robber-gang: "What do you do if you see a great opportunity to steal on a Sabbath?" "We steal on the Sabbath," said the robber. "And what if it involves lighting a candle on a Sabbath?" asked the rabbi. "Then we light it," said the robber. "And what do you do if you have a chance to steal a pig?" asked the rabbi. "Then we steal it," answered the thug. "And what do you do with it?" asked the rabbi. "We sell it," answered the thief. "Why don't you eat it?" asked the rabbi. "Because we Jews shouldn't eat pork," said the robber. "But Jewish law does not permit you to rob or strike a light on the Sabbath, and you still do it...." "Rabbi," said the robber, "all those are part of our way of life, that's how we make our living. But how can we eat pork? We are still Jews."

Jewish history is filled with stories of Jews who refused to violate the dietary laws under extreme pressure and persecution or even threats of death. Jewish dietary laws are much more than ancient health measures. The philosophical and ethical ideas behind these laws are rooted in biblical and rabbinic ordinances that distinguish between permissible (*kosher*) and forbidden (*trefah*) foods. Moses Maimonides, the great medieval Jewish thinker, said that the Jewish dietary laws serve to control Jews' appetites and keep them from thinking that food and drink are the only purpose in life.

Jews are commanded to keep the dietary laws mainly for spiritual reasons: "For I am the Lord your God; sanctify yourself and be holy, for I am holy" (Leviticus 11:44). The laws permit Jews to eat meat but only the flesh of animals that are cloven-footed and chew cud: cattle, sheep, goat, and deer. Water animals that have both fins and scales are permitted. Birds of prey and reptiles are forbidden, as is animal blood. A kosher slaughterer, or *shochet*, slaughters the animal—*shechita*—which must also be checked for diseases. Jews are forbidden to eat meat and dairy products at the same meal, and observant families have two sets of dishes to avoid mixing the two. They also keep two sinks for preparing and clearing away meals, making sure that no meat touches the dairy dishes and vice versa.

SABBATH AND FESTIVALS

Before a festival, anticipation settles over the Jewish household. Spirits perk up weeks in advance. Special tasks occupy the community—food shopping, cooking, buying new clothes for the children, sending invitations to festive meals. "Everyday" gives way to "holiday," and then the Jewish world rests.

The Torah mentions six major holidays: Passover, Shavuot, Rosh Hashana, Yom Kippur, Sukkot, and Shmini Atzeret. The first and seventh days of Passover, the first day of Sukkot, and the days of Shavuot, Shmini Atzeret, and Rosh Hashanah are sacred days during which no work may be done. By rabbinical edict, Jews celebrate Rosh Hashanah for two days. In the Diaspora, an extra day was added to each of the festivals, so that the first and last two days of Passover, two days of Shavuot, the first two days of Sukkot, and two days of Shmini Atzeret are observed in orthodox and most traditional circles. The fast of Yom Kippur is celebrated both in Israel and elsewhere for one day.

The reason why some Jews celebrate holidays for two days is rooted in a history that is at once practical and colorful. In ancient days, a holiday's date was judged according to the time the new moon, which signaled the new month, was first spotted. Jews all over the world lit bonfires on hilltops to announce the day. Later, messengers ran from one community to the next. They could not always get to distant places in time to announce the correct day and therefore a second day was added. This addition of a second day became the norm from the second century on for communities outside of Israel.

51

The candles are lit for a Friday evening meal.

From the Dictionnaire Historique. . . de la Bible *(Paris, 1730), this illustration is of a Jewish synagogue on the Sabbath.*

The Sabbath

שבת

Six days shall you labor and do all your work; but the seventh day is a Sabbath unto the Lord your God. In it you shall not do any manner of work. . . for the Lord blessed the Sabbath day and sanctified it.
(*Exodus 20:9–11*)

She is called Queen Sabbath, Bride Sabbath: graceful, peaceful, and beautiful. Beginning at sunset each Friday and lasting until approximately an hour after sunset Saturday, the Sabbath is a spiritual day when each person should look deep into his soul. It is a day of communion between man and his creator. The Sabbath is the only commandment among the ten given to Moses that deals directly with a ritual observance; it holds a special meaning in Jewish life.

Preparations for the welcoming of Queen Sabbath—cleaning, shopping, and cooking—can start Thursday evening. Special meals are prepared. Freshly laundered clothes are set aside to be worn on the Sabbath.

Early on Friday, the family returns from work or school to bathe, shave, and dress for Sabbath. A white tablecloth is spread on the table, which is then set with special Sabbath dishes. Prepared in advance, the food is different from everyday meals, and guests are often invited.

On the first Sabbath after her marriage, a Jewish wife begins lighting the Sabbath candles for her family. Eighteen minutes before sundown, dressed in her best clothes, the mother of the house lights at least two candles symbolizing the two versions in the Torah of the Fourth Commandment: *Zachor* ("*Remember* the Sabbath day to keep it holy") and *Shamor* ("*Observe* the Sabbath day to keep it holy"). "Blessed art Thou," says the wife, "Lord our God, King of the universe, Who has sanctified us with His commandments and commanded us to kindle the Sabbath lights." "Amen," answers the family, gathered around the woman of the house. "*Shabat Shalom*," a peaceful Sabbath, they wish each other. Queen Sabbath now reigns.

After the candles are lit, the men of the family go to synagogue for the Welcoming of the Sabbath (*Kabbalat Shabbat*) and the evening prayer. When they return, the family gathers around the table and sings a welcoming song for the Sabbath: "Peace on you, angels of the Most High. . . . Bless me with peace, angels of peace, angels of the Most High. . . ."

The spirit of the holy day permeates the house. Children stay close to their parents, and the father, placing his hands on his children's bowed heads, recites to his sons: "May God make you as Ephraim and Menasheh" and to his daughters: "May God make you as Sarah, Rebecca, Rachel, and Leah." To both he says, "May the Lord bless you and protect you. May the Lord shine His countenance upon you and be gracious to you. May the Lord favor you and grant you peace."

The head of the household next holds up the *Kiddush* cup, filled with sweet red wine, and says the Sabbath Kiddush on behalf of those gathered: "Blessed art Thou, Lord our God, King of the universe, Who has sanctified us with His Commandments and has been pleased with us; in love and favor has given us His holy Sabbath as a heritage, a memorial of the creation—that day being also the first among the holy festivals, in remembrance of the exodus from Egypt. Thou hast chosen us and hallowed us above all nations, and in love and favor hast given us the holy Sabbath as a heritage. Blessed art Thou, O Lord, Who hallowest the Sabbath." "Amen," answers the gathering. The head of the household then drinks from the cup and passes it along to his loved ones, sharing the wine of blessing. A Sabbath bond unites the table. Family members wash their hands, reciting a special prayer. They are now ready for the Sabbath dinner.

Two intertwined Sabbath loaves of *challah* are covered and placed on the table. Before they are cut and distributed, a prayer is said: "Blessed art Thou, Lord our God, King of the universe, Who brings forth bread from the earth." The two loaves, like the candles, symbolize the two forms of the Fourth Commandment, but they also represent the extra portion of manna that was provided to the Israelites in the desert.

Most Ashkenazic families start their Sabbath meals with boiled fish cakes (gefilte fish), followed by chicken soup. Between courses, they sing songs telling of the greatness of the Sabbath, which add a festive atmosphere to the holy day.

Even today in North African Jewish households, the Sabbath's beautiful colors and sounds start two days before the actual day. The women of the house, who organize most of the Sabbath preparations, start shopping for food on Wednesday. The men bring sweets and goodies, which include a garland of myrtle and jasmine used for the blessing of the scents after the Kiddush. In fact, many North African Jews who now live in Israel plant myrtle and jasmine in their gardens specifically for the Sabbath. Meal preparation begins in earnest on Friday morning and lasts until an hour and a half before sundown.

Some North African families light only one Sabbath candle, which is placed on a small plate on a special shelf. The men of the household go to synagogue while the women stay home. When the men return, they say a prayer to bless the peaceful Sabbath and sing a special song—*Eishet Chail*—praising the mother of the house. This song is sung in Ashkenazic households as well. The family gathers around the table and recites the blessings of the scents. If a member of the family is absent, North African Jews recite a special prayer, hoping for that person to show up on the following Sabbath. After the Kiddush, everyone kisses the hand of the oldest person present. "God bless you," that person says in return.

53

Even now, when most North African Jews have moved to various other parts of the world, a traditional Sabbath dinner begins with a large variety of fresh and cooked salads, home-baked breads, and wines. Couscous, a dish of crushed wheat, is served with meatballs, followed by a selection of fruits. Tunisian Jews never serve fish for the Sabbath dinner; it is considered a poor man's food. In Algerian Jews' houses, on the other hand, fish is usually the main course for every Sabbath dinner.

Jews all over the world enjoy their leisure on this day of rest, walking to synagogue, meeting in study groups, gathering with friends. No work may be done. "Work," defined by Jewish law as any act of creative control over nature, includes driving, switching on lights, and cooking. (Many Jews do drive and use electricity on the Sabbath). Heated foods are kept warm on a special hot plate. After the Sabbath morning services, a Kiddush is again recited, and another meal is served. A total of three meals are served over the course of the Sabbath.

Historically in Tunisia, after the father came home from Saturday morning prayers, the family ate a special Sabbath stew, *hamin*, a dish that was cooked overnight on a small fire. (Today, many North American Jews also enjoy hamin [known also as *cholent*] on the Sabbath.) Before the stew, the family feasted on eggs that were cooked in the stew. Families could also celebrate by going to one of the Jewish coffee shops in Tunisia that were kept open on the Sabbath and being served a special menu of hamin and various drinks. It was the custom to pay for the meal the next day, as observant Jews do not handle money on the Sabbath.

On Friday, a Kiddush *cup (above) is filled with wine and held by the head of the household, who recites the Sabbath* Kiddush.

An embroidered ceremonial cloth (above) is used to cover the challah.

55

Spice boxes and candle holders are used in the Havdalah *ceremony at the end of the Sabbath.*
The above artifacts are from Germany and date from the sixteenth to eighteenth centuries.

Libyan Jews used to celebrate the Sabbath with couscous and a dish called *mafrum*, richly seasoned meatballs made with parsley and sandwiched between slices of egg and potatoes or eggplant.

Even today, Moroccan Jews eat a small meal right after completing their Sabbath preparations. After lighting the oil candles, the family drinks a liquor and blesses the food. This light meal is called B*o'i Kala*, which means, ''Come in, bride.'' Moroccan Jews also eat *hamin*, which they call *adofina*, on the Sabbath; they say, ''A Sabbath without adofina is like a king without a kingdom.''

When three bright stars are spotted in the Saturday evening sky, the Sabbath is over. Jews then welcome a new week with the H*avdalah* ceremony. Blessings are recited over a cup of wine, over fragrant spices (*besamim*) that symbolize a sweet week, and over the light of the candles. The fragrant smell of the spices is regarded by rabbinic sources as a delight to the soul, making up for the additional soul that was added to every human being for the Sabbath but is now leaving. ''Blessed art Thou, Lord our God, King of the universe, Who makes a distinction between the sacred and secular, between light and darkness, between Israel and the other nations, between the seventh day and the six working days. Blessed art Thou, Lord, Who makes a distinction between the sacred and the secular.'' After the Havdalah, the song about Elijah the prophet is sung. Elijah, traditionally the herald of the Messiah, is invited to come and bring the Messiah.

Passover

In the temperate climates when kids and lambs are born, flowers bloom, and the smell of blossoms perfumes the fields, the Jewish world celebrates Passover. The Anniversary of Redemption, Feast of Freedom, Festival of the Unleavened Bread, Celebration of Spring—the oldest holiday of them all, Pesach.

"Let my people go," Moses cried to Pharaoh Ramses II. Pharaoh's repeated refusals brought upon himself and the Egyptians ten plagues, ten divinely made catastrophes: blood (that is, their water turned to blood), frogs, lice, wild beasts, blight, boils, hail, locusts, darkness, and slaying of the firstborn. The last plague broke Pharaoh's spirit and convinced him to let the Israelites leave his country. This event stands as the focal point of Jewish history. The Exodus crystallized the Jewish national identity and marked the birth of the free Jewish nation.

Pesach begins on the evening of the fourteenth day of the Jewish month of Nisan and lasts for eight days. It celebrates the deliverance of the Children of Israel from more than two centuries of Egyptian bondage. God promised to exempt, or "pass over," the Jewish houses in Egypt while striking down the Egyptian firstborn children, so the celebration was named Passover.

And the Children of Israel escaped. In their haste to leave behind Egyptian oppression, afraid that Pharaoh would change his mind, they baked bread without giving it time to rise. In remembrance of that event, Jews are not permitted to eat—or own—any leavened bread or any food containing leavening during Passover. Such foods are called *hametz*, and include wheat, rye, barley, oats, and spelt that have soaked in water for at least eighteen minutes. The Torah prescribes *matzo* (unleavened bread) in place of bread: "Seven days shall you eat unleavened bread. . . . Seven days shall there be no leaven found in your house; for whoever eats what is leavened, that person shall be cut off from the congregation. . . ." (Exodus 12:15,19).

A buzz fills the air for weeks before the holiday. So many preparations to be done, decisions to be made, and activities to perform. Every Jewish home needs a thorough housecleaning: windows, doors, carpets. Fresh liner paper may be spread on the shelves where hametz was stored (before the holiday, shoppers are careful not to purchase any hametz). New furniture may be purchased, and new clothes chosen for the children. Passover dinnerware is taken out and washed. Ovens and utensils are made kosher for Passover. A special joy settles over each Jewish community.

On the evening before the first day of Passover, Jews recite: "Blessed art Thou, Lord our God, King of the universe Who has commanded us concerning the removal of the hametz." Holding a lighted candle, the head of the household moves through the darkened house, looking for any offending crumbs of bread. Searching each shadowy room, guided only by a candle, is a memorable experience for both young and old. If any hametz is found, it is collected and wrapped safely for burning the following day. Then someone says: "All leaven and all hametz that is in my possession that I did not see and did not destroy, let it be null and ownerless as the dust of the earth."

On the following morning, any hametz that was located is thrown into a bonfire. Jews in modern times who find themselves with large quantities of hametz and who do not wish to lose their costly goods sell it to non-Jews just before the holiday, the conditions of sale allowing the Jew to buy it back after the holiday concludes.

The order of the dinner—the word seder *means "order"—and recitations, songs, and prayers are written in the* Haggadah. *The book's name stems from the Hebrew word for* tell *because it tells the story of the Israelites' exodus from Egypt.*

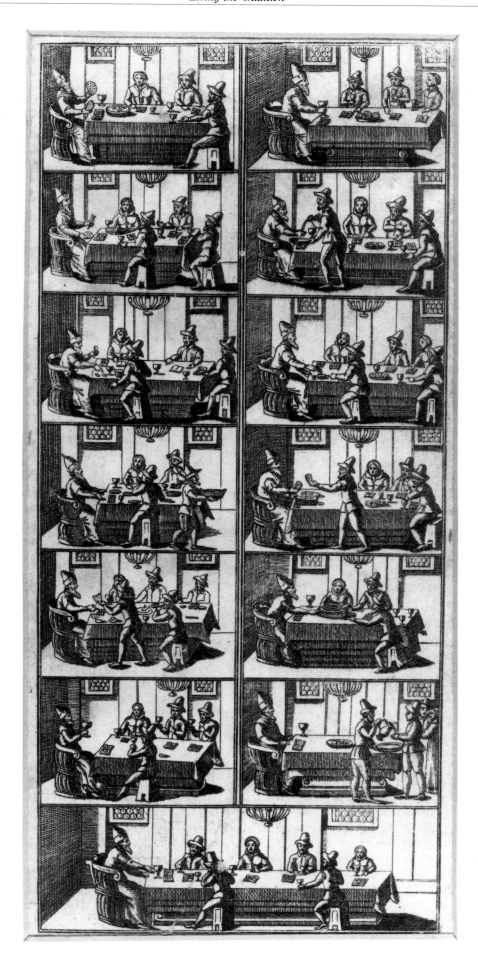

GEORGE GERSHWIN *(1898–1937)*

Born in New York, composer George Gershwin wrote his first song while working in a music publishing house in the famous "Tin Pan Alley." His first great hit, "Swanee," sung by Al Jolson in the musical *Sinbad* in 1918, established him as one of the United States' greatest composers.

Gershwin's original and modern composition style won him the attention of both audiences and critics when he wrote *Rhapsody in Blue*. This jazz symphony, written in 1924, placed jazz on a concert stage for the first time.

Although Gershwin had almost no formal musical education, he wrote many songs that have since become classics. His brother, Ira, wrote most of the lyrics. They collaborated on such Broadway musicals as *Lady Be Good, Strike Up the Band, Girl Crazy, Oh Kay!,* and *Of Thee I Sing,* the first musical to win a Pulitzer Prize.

Gershwin's most famous Broadway show was written in 1934. *Porgy and Bess,* a remarkable musical drama that deals with ghetto and race relations between the inhabitants of Catfish Row and a crippled beggar who cares for a beautiful but reckless girl, was composed under the influence of both cantorial and black music, a combination that created a haunting and lasting emotional experience. The movie version of this show brought Gershwin's music to even more Americans.

These illustrations from an 1878 Haggadah *printed in Livorno, Italy, show a housewife making preparations for Passover.*

CHAIM SOUTINE *(1893–1943)*

Although he lived a short life, Chaim Soutine was one of the most important painters of his era. Born in Lithuania to the family of a poor tailor, he ran away from home at the age of eleven. He went to Minsk and then to Vilna, where he studied at the School of Fine Arts.

In 1913, a wealthy physician recognized his great talent and gave him the money he needed to go to Paris. There he met Amadeo Modigliani, who liked his work and tried to help him. At one point the two painters shared living space and took turns sleeping in the only bed in the room.

Paris was not easy on the suffering artist. Soutine financed himself by copying Old Masters at the Louvre, working as a porter, and digging ditches. In despair, he tried at one point to commit suicide. His situation improved after the dying Modigliani introduced him to an art dealer who brought an American collector to his studio. The collector bought fifty of Soutine's paintings, and his reputation spread to England and the United States.

Refusing to leave France when the Nazis occupied the country, Soutine was forced into hiding in a small village in Touraine. Fear and anxiety caused a severe ulcer attack, and in 1943, he died in a Paris hospital after undergoing an operation.

Soutine painted the people and places of Western Europe. He never used his ghetto background as an influence in his paintings. He is considered to be one of the great Expressionists. His paintings are filled with violent, almost bleeding colors, reflecting his own agonized and troubled soul.

59

On the first day of Passover, a white tablecloth is spread on the dinner table in preparation for the special religious service and holiday meal—the *seder*. Bottles of red wine shine, waiting to be drunk. Each adult participant must drink four symbolic cups of wine over the course of the seder. The four cups signify the four expressions used in the Torah to describe Israel's redemption: "I will *bring* you out from under the burdens of the Egyptians"; "I will *deliver* you from their bondage"; "I will *redeem* you with an outstretched arm and with great judgments"; and "I will *take* you to me for a people, and I will be to you God" (Exodus 6:6–7).

Specific foods also take on symbolic meaning. On a special Passover plate placed in the middle of the table are set a green vegetable called *karpas*, usually celery or parsley; *maror* or bitter herbs, generally freshly grated horseradish or romaine lettuce, that serve as a reminder of the bitterness endured by the Jews during their slavery in Egypt; *haroset*, a mixture of chopped apples and nuts with wine and spices, a reminder of the mortar that was used by the Jewish slaves to build the Egyptian cities; and a roasted shankbone (*z'roa*) and roasted egg (*beitzah*) to remind Jews of the offerings that were brought when the Temple existed. Although not on the seder plate, dishes of saltwater are scattered around the table, for the custom dictates that all who participate must dip the parsley into the salty water, a symbol for the tears shed during the enslavement.

Also in the middle of the table, usually made of silver or gold and beautifully engraved, shines the cup of Elijah the prophet. This is the fifth cup—which is not drunk from—representing the promise of, and Jews' faith in, the coming of the Messiah. Three matzos, covered with a special ceremonial cover, are placed at the head of the table before the conductor of the seder.

The order of the dinner—*seder* means "order"—and its recitations, songs, and prayers are written in the *Haggadah*, a book whose name stems from the Hebrew word for *tell* because it tells the story of the Israelites' exodus from Egypt. As it is a great command, or *mitzvah*, to tell the story of this heroic Jewish escape from the hands of their oppressors, families sit around the table till the late hours of the night each year, singing and relating the history of the enslavement and the

These two Passover plates are from the Museum of the Old Cemetery in Prague.

exodus. Different versions of telling the story developed over the centuries, and different communities created diverse ways to celebrate. The birth of the State of Israel and migration of Jews of all backgrounds into this melting pot helped to blend these various customs.

Through the years, various customs became incorporated into the *Haggadah* in order to make it more lively and involve the youngsters in the ceremony. For instance, one of the matzos is broken in half early in the evening, and the head of the household customarily hides one half, the *afikoman*, somewhere in the house. During the course of the evening, the children must find the missing piece, for which they are rewarded. Children are also encouraged to ask questions, a practice that has become ritual; the youngest literate member of the family traditionally recites or sings the "Four Questions," beginning with "Why is this night different from all other nights?"

In the past, Tunisian Jews started preparing for Passover a month before the holiday. All the dishes that were served during Passover were special. On the thirteenth day of the month, each family slaughtered a lamb; one family member dipped his hand in the animal's blood and spread it on the front of the house, just as the Jews did in Egypt long ago following God's command (in order to distinguish their houses from the houses of the Egyptians). Lamb meat, rice, and green beans adorned the table.

During the seder, various foods are used to symbolize the experience of the Israelites in Egypt.

Raisa Robbins' 1947 painting
Passover Night.

ה7

מהו אומ מה זאת ואמרת
אליו בחוק יד הוציאנו יי
ממצרים מבית עבדים

ויאמר

These are pages from the Spanish Prato Haggadah, circa 1300.

SARAH BERNHARDT *(1844–1923)*

The French actress Sarah Bernhardt was born Henriette Rasine Bernard. The Paris stage star, who was called by writer Victor Hugo "The Divine Sarah," was the illegitimate daughter of a Dutch Jewish mother and a French father. Bernhardt was the leading lady of the famous Comédie Française and was especially well known for her roles in Racine's plays.

In 1879, Bernhardt formed her own company and toured the world, playing to enthusiastic audiences. When she returned to Paris, she acted in three of Sardon's plays. Her fans were charmed by her melodic voice and gracious gestures. She became a legend in her own time, and her name became synonymous with dramatic acting. When she was seventy years old, her right leg was amputated, but she continued to perform despite her ill health. Bernhardt also directed the Sarah Bernhardt Theater, which opened in 1899, and remained active until she died while working on a film.

JASCHA HEIFETZ *(1901–)*

Born in the town of Vilna in Lithuania, Jascha Heifetz started playing the violin at the age of three under his father's tutelage. He played the Mendelssohn violin concerto in public when he was seven and at ten entered the St. Petersburg Conservatory. One year later, he played with the Berlin Philharmonic Orchestra. At the outbreak of the Russian Revolution, his family immigrated to America via Siberia and Japan. In the United States, his playing reached an early perfection, characterized by an aristocratic restraint and setting a new style of violin playing.

Heifetz performed throughout the world, including Russia and, in 1925, Palestine. When he played with the Israel Philharmonic Orchestra in 1950, Heifetz was attacked physically and slightly injured because he chose to include a piece by Richard Strauss (whose work was not played in Israel because of his association with Hitler and the Nazis). He has arranged a number of works for the violin, and in later years he retreated into semi-retirement.

66

The most interesting customs occurred on the first seder evening. (Traditional Jews in the Diaspora conduct seders on the first two nights.) After the Kiddush, one of the family members traditionally held the Passover plate high over the guests' heads and circled the table three times. During the dinner, unlike their counterparts in Ashkenazi communities, children in Tunisia did not ask the Four Questions, and some communities did not practice the ritual of searching for the afikoman. Instead, at the end of the seder dinner, the head of the household served each participant two pieces from the afikoman, one on top of the other. Each member had to eat the upper part and keep the second part all year long as a charm for good fortune. The mother of the house also kept some of the haroset to "glue" it to one of the door lintels after the holiday. The seder would last well into the night; during these late hours, with children often asleep on their chairs, Arab friends of the family might come in to listen to the beautiful songs that concluded the seder. Tunisian Jews kept the door open to admit Elijah the prophet and any other guest who might come.

In Libyan Jewish communities, one of the family members wrapped a piece of the afikoman in a napkin, put it on his shoulder, and left the room while the children yelled, "Thief, thief!" When the family member returned, the father of the family would ask, "Where have you been?" and he would answer, "In Egypt." "And where are you going?" "To Jerusalem," came the response. The family would then say, "Next year in Jerusalem" three times and start reading the *Haggadah*.

Moroccan seders of the past included a custom unfamiliar to most Westerners. Right after the Four Questions, the seder conductor left the room, then returned through a side door, leaning on a walking stick and carrying the afikoman, wrapped in a napkin or kerchief, on his shoulder. He would tell the guests gathered around

ALBERT EINSTEIN *(1879–1955)*

Albert Einstein, father of the theory of relativity, is the most prominent physicist of modern times. Born in Germany, he published four early papers that caught the attention of leading physicists around the world and led to his appointment as professor in three major European universities.

After his work was authenticated, he was awarded the Nobel Prize for physics. He left Nazi Germany to find refuge in the United States, where his scientific discoveries set the ground for nuclear theory and the development of the atomic bomb.

The United States embraced Einstein, and his famous letter to President Roosevelt alerted Americans to the potential hazards of atomic weapons.

Einstein was not only a brilliant scientist but also a devoted humanitarian. He was sympathetic to Zionist ideas and proud of his Jewishness, and donated a great deal of time to helping the State of Israel in general and the Hebrew University in Jerusalem in particular. After the death of Israel's first president, Chaim Weizmann, Einstein was invited to serve as the country's honorary president, but he refused the offer in order to continue with his scientific studies.

NORMAN MAILER *(1923–)*

Norman Mailer, U.S. novelist and essayist, was born in New Jersey and graduated from Harvard University. His service in the United States Army during World War II was the background for his best-selling novel *The Naked and the Dead*, published in 1948, in which he managed to capture the fear and despair of men at war. The different sides within people and their drive to extremes fascinated Mailer, and he tried, as much as possible, to deal in his writing with people who were caught in difficult and extreme situations. Feeling limited within the framework of the novel, he dedicated himself to improving the form of the essay to the point of perfection. In 1968, his brilliantly written eyewitness account of an anti–Vietnam War demonstration in Washington, D.C., entitled *The Armies in the Night*, won a Pulitzer Prize and established Norman Mailer as perhaps the greatest writer in the United States.

67

the table that he was one of the Children of Israel who had just witnessed God's great miracle of parting the Red Sea; he told how the matzo was baked in a rush.

For Moroccan Jews living in Israel or other countries, the original rituals have changed a bit. Jews of Moroccan origin now living outside of Morocco do not eat rice and legumes, as do other North African and Yemenite Jews (but not Ashkenazic Jews).

Mimuna is a special celebration of friendship that takes place on the night after the eighth day of Passover in Morocco. Neither meat nor coffee is served on the eve of the Mimuna. The door to the house is left open for anybody who wants to enter. No one is asked his identity, and each and every guest is welcomed with a greeting and a wish of good luck. Tables groan with spreads of coconut pastries, caramel, sesame cakes, and jams of all kinds. A large bowl filled with flour is set in the middle of the table, and members of the household dust their gold jewelry with it as a symbol for a fruitful year. Some families leave the gold and flour out for eight days, hoping for a year of prosperity.

Fish swim in a bowl filled with water and mint leaves—symbolizing the hope that the nation will be fertile and the Jewish people will multiply like fish. Men and women wear traditional clothing, and the women prepare *muflta*, pancakes covered with honey and butter.

Although the celebration in Morocco lasted into the wee hours, it was considered lucky to get up as early as possible in the morning: people often rose early and went to the beach to see seven waves—to remember the parting of the Red Sea. Also a single woman was supposed to put her feet in the water, trusting that this would bring her a joyful wedding the following year. After returning from the shore, the celebrators visited with friends.

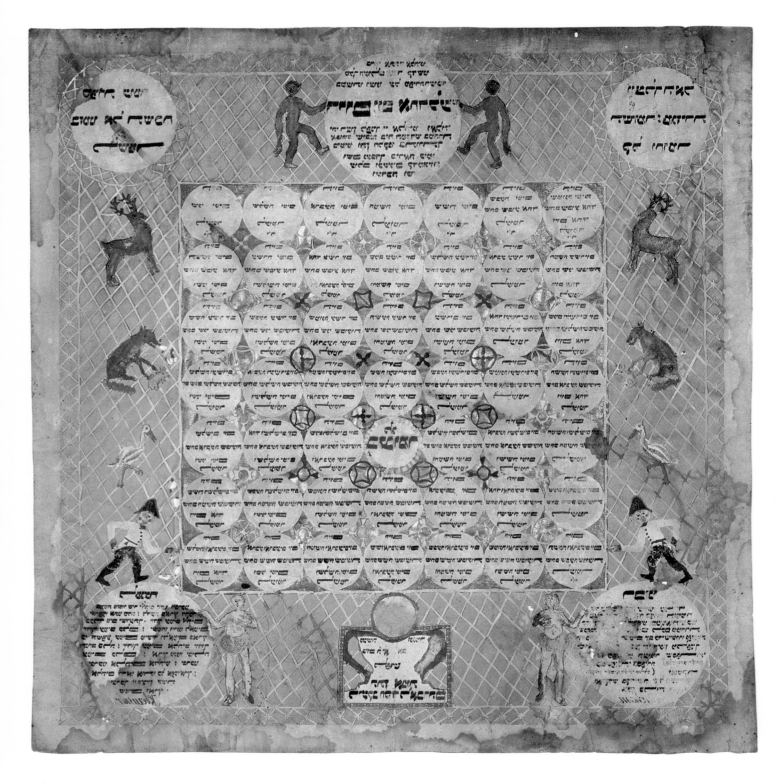

This Jewish calendar from Italy is used to count the omer, *which ties the festival of Passover with the festival of Shavuot.*

Shavuot

From the day after the day of rest, the day that you bring the sheaf of wave offering, you shall keep count for seven full weeks; you shall count fifty days, until the day after the seventh week . . . there shall be a holy convocation to you; you shall do no manner of servile work.
(*Leviticus 23:15–16, 21*)

שבועות

Traditionally, Shavuot is the holiday that celebrates the Torah being given to the People of Israel. This depiction is from the Sefer **Minhagim** *(the Book of Customs, Amsterdam, 1723).*

69

Seven weeks after the exodus from Egypt, God revealed himself to the Children of Israel at Mount Sinai. According to Jewish tradition the Ten Commandments, the moral foundation for all of Western civilization, and the entire Torah were presented there. The festival of Shavuot stresses that release from bondage and political oppression is not real freedom and is incomplete unless it culminates in reverence for God and respect for others, as taught to the Children of Israel in God's revelation on Mount Sinai.

Shavuot, the Festival of Weeks and the Feast of the Harvest, is celebrated on the sixth day of the Jewish month of Sivan. Orthodox and Conservative Jews in North America observe it for two days, while Reform Jews and Jews in Israel celebrate for one day only. It is a celebration of balm, a festival that also symbolizes the end of the grain harvest.

In ancient Israel, the beginning of the grain harvest was marked by a sacrifice of the *omer*, the first sheaf of the newly cut barley, at the sanctuary. Farmers gathered this first harvest and made the sometimes long journey to Jerusalem. Fifty days later, at the close of the harvest period, two loaves of bread baked from newly ground wheat, or any of the first fruits of the harvest (*bikkurim*), were offered as a sacrifice.

Beginning with the second night of Passover, Jews start the counting of the omer (*sefirat haomer*) to commemorate this cycle. The counting of the omer ties the festival of Passover with the festival of Shavuot. During the thirty-three-day period of sefirat haomer, thousands of followers of the great Rabbi Akiva died of plague in the second century. Since then, the thirty-three days of the omer are considered semi-mourning days. Jews will not cut their hair during this period nor will they schedule a wedding, and celebrations with music are forbidden.

With the rebirth of the State of Israel, kibbutz members reenact the omer cycle. They dress in white and decorate their wagons with hay and greenery; children carry baskets filled with fresh fruits. At the center of the kibbutz, on a large, decorated platform, an older member plays the role of the high priest. The gathering sings, and the children bring their harvest to the "priest."

The eve of Shavuot is a *leil shimurim*, a night of study. All night long, many Jewish men study and pray in the house of study, the *beit hamidrash*. The morning's breakfast consists of dairy dishes, as do all meals on this holiday. Eating dairy commemorates the Israelites' return to their tents after receiving the Torah; they were too tired and hungry to wait for meat to be cooked. The second night of Shavuot is spent reading the Psalms of David, as tradition says that King David died on Shavuot.

When living in Morocco, Jews used to pour water on themselves during Shavuot, actively symbolizing that the Torah is like fresh water to the thirsty spirit. On the morning of the festival, Libyan Jews traditionally handed each child fresh water and seven small leaves from a thorn bush, which stood for the burning bush. (God first spoke to Moses from a burning bush, so Shavuot, the Torah, and the bush are linked symbolically. The number seven refers to the number of weeks between Passover [the exodus] and Shavuot [the giving of the Torah].)

70

BEVERLY SILLS *(1929–   )*

Born in Brooklyn, New York, Belle Miriam Silverman always knew that she would be an opera star. The Woman of the Year in Performing Arts for 1975 is one of the most gracious, famous, and well-established artists in the world of opera.

Sills began her career on Major Bowes Amateur Hour. She went on to sing bit parts in radio soap operas and on a national tour in a Gilbert and Sullivan show. When she was cast in the American opera *The Ballad of Baby Doe*, she marked her first great success on the opera stage.

Sills continued singing classical roles at the New York City Opera and rose to the status of a great star. Rave reviews have followed her performances, and her bubbly personality has made her a lovable and admired figure all over the world. She has been on the cover of *Time* and *Newsweek* magazines, and in 1975 her long-awaited debut at the Metropolitan Opera House in New York was covered as a major media event. Sills retired from the stage to become Artistic Director of the New York City Opera. She continues to be a popular guest on television shows and an important personality in the world of classical music.

ISAAC ASIMOV *(1920–1992)*

A biochemist and author who was born in the U.S.S.R., Isaac Asimov came to the United States at the age of three. He graduated from Columbia with a Ph.D. in 1948 and taught at Boston University Medical School and became an associate professor of biochemistry. His work in enzymology is as highly regarded as his literary achievements.

Since 1950 Asimov wrote books ranging from serious science texts (*A Short History of Chemistry* and *The Wellsprings of Life*) to such science-fiction classics as *I Robot*, *The Cave of Steel*, and *The Foundation Trilogy*.

Rosh Hashanah

According to tradition, Creation took place on the first of the Jewish month of Tishrei, which became known as the New Year, Rosh Hashanah. "And the Lord spoke unto Moses saying: 'Speak unto the children of Israel saying: In the seventh month, in the first day of the month, shall be a solemn rest unto you, a memorial proclaimed with the blast of horns, a holy convocation" (Leviticus 23:23–24).

Three books are opened on Rosh Hashanah. One is for the out-and-out wicked, the second for the truly righteous, and the third is for those in between. The righteous are immediately inscribed for life, the wicked for death. All those in the middle are sentenced on Yom Kippur.

Rosh Hashanah, called in the Torah the Day of Remembrance (*Yom Hazikaron*) and the Day of Sounding the Shofar (*Yom Teruah*), begins a ten-day period of spiritual elevation, self-examination, and testing. It is marked by intense prayers, acceptance and acknowledgment of God's rule over the world, and a special closeness to the Creator of the world. On Rosh Hashanah, it is believed, God judges all human beings. Ten days later, on Yom Kippur, people's fates are sealed by the Almighty.

71

In the Torah, Rosh Hashanah is called the Day of Sounding the Shofar.

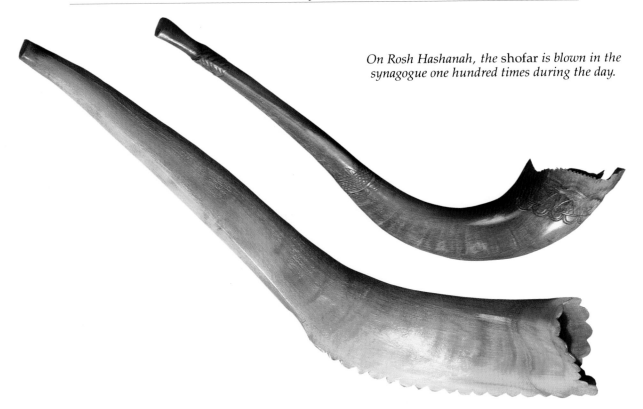

On Rosh Hashanah, the shofar *is blown in the synagogue one hundred times during the day.*

72

The blowing of the shofar *(above) during the High Holidays is portrayed on this New Year's card.*

This New Year's greeting card (above), Shana Tovah, *describes the need to sacrifice your life for the love of the Lord.*

*The sound of the shofar heard during the High Holidays of Rosh Hashanah and Yom Kippur
serves as a reminder of the ancient shofar heard at Sinai.*

On the eve of Rosh Hashanah, the synagogue is filled with men and women of all ages. People wish one another a happy new year, and add, "May you be inscribed for a good year." A spirit of holiness prevails.

Afterward, members of the community retreat to their homes for a holiday meal. After Kiddush, this festive dinner usually begins with dipping an apple in honey as a wish for a sweet year to come: "May it be the Lord's will to renew for us a year that will be good and sweet."

To this day, North African Jews empty their salt shakers, fill them with sugar, and leave them open for the day. Tunisian Jews serve only sweet dishes: sesame seeds in honey, cookies, halvah, pomegranate seeds, jams, and pieces of apple and garlic dipped in honey. After eating the sweet appetizers, the family sings holiday songs and then proceeds to the second course of broad beans (which symbolize wealth) and pasta with meat.

The first day of Rosh Hashanah is devoted to prayers. The community gathers again in the synagogue, prays, and listens to the shofar. Fear and awe grip the worshipers as the ark of the Torah is opened and the cantor sings the sacred prayer *Unetaneh Tokef.*

These New Year's cards, created in "relief" (an art form that was popular in the nineteenth century), depict scenes from the synagogue at Rosh Hashanah.

HENRIETTA SZOLD *(1860–1945)*

Henrietta Szold, the founder of Hadassah (the Women's Zionist Organization of America), was born in Baltimore, Maryland, and started her career as a teacher. She then worked as part of the American Zionist Medical Unit for Palestine, which brought her to Palestine in 1929, where she became the director of the School of Nursing in Jerusalem.

While in Jerusalem, she helped form the Hadassah University Hospital and the Alice Seligsberg Trade School for Girls. When the Nazis came to power, Szold was appointed director of *Aliyat Hanoar* (Youth Aliyah), the immigration and rehabilitation organization for young boys and girls from Germany. *Aliyat Hanoar* helped thousands of youngsters who had fled the Nazis to resettle in Israel.

The Youth Aliyah movement, Henrietta Szold's "baby," continues to operate today, helping misplaced children from all over the world to adjust to their new lives and function in their new homes in Israel. Kibbutz Kfar Szold, established by a group of German graduates of Youth Aliyah, was named in Henrietta Szold's honor.

We will declare the greatness and the holiness of this day, for thereon Thy kingdom is exalted, Thy throne established in mercy, and Thou judgest in truth. It is true that Thou art the judge; Thou reprovest; Thou knowest all; Thou bearest witness, recordest and sealest. . . . How many are to pass away, and how many are to come into existence; who are to live and who are to die; who are to accomplish the full number of their days, and who are not to accomplish them; who are to perish by water and who by fire, who by the sword and who by thunder; who by earthquake and who by plagues; who shall have repose and who shall be troubled; who shall be tranquil and who shall be disturbed; who shall be prosperous and who shall be afflicted; who shall become poor and who shall become rich; who shall be cast down and who shall be exalted.

After the midday meal, some Jews—children and adults, men and women, all dressed in festive clothing—go to the nearest river or other streams of water to perform *tashlich*. As they recite special prayers, they empty their pockets or throw bread upon the water, thus symbolically discarding their sins.

Israel stops its usual activity on Rosh Hashanah. All work ceases, and Jews attend services in their synagogues and listen to the blare of the shofar, which is blown one hundred times during the day. The sound of the shofar serves as a reminder of the ancient shofar heard at Sinai.

76

Dating from the early eighteenth century, this Rosh Hashanah plate is from Bells, Holland.

AVRAHAM GOLDFADEN *(1840–1908)*

Avraham Goldfaden, dramatist and composer, is considered the father of the Yiddish theater. Born in the Ukraine, Goldfaden received a thorough Hebrew education and also studied Russian, German, and other secular subjects.

To avoid being drafted into the Russian army, Goldfaden was sent to a government school at the age of fifteen, where he met Abraham Ber Gottlober, a teacher who influenced him greatly. When he entered a rabbinical seminary, he was encouraged to develop his writing skills, and he started publishing songs in both Hebrew and Yiddish. His first collection of Yiddish songs was published in 1866 after he graduated from the seminary.

In 1875, Goldfaden moved to Romania, where he met a group of Jewish entertainers, the Broder Brothers, who started singing his material. A year later, he formed his first theater group, a combination of wandering minstrels and actors, and toured Romania with great success. By 1880, his company had toured all over Russia. Under Goldfaden's influence, Yiddish theater grew and flourished in Russia until 1883, when the government banned all plays performed in the Yiddish language.

In 1882 Goldfaden went to New York. Finding the competition too great, he decided to produce and direct his plays in London, Paris, and other European cities first. In 1903 he returned to the United States, where he spent his last five years. Some of his plays, such as *The Two Kuni Lemels* and *Shulamit*, are still produced. His music and songs, such as "Rozhinkes mit Mandlen" (Raisins and Almonds), are also still performed and are considered classics.

FRANZ KAFKA *(1883–1924)*

German novelist Franz Kafka was born in Czechoslovakia. Raised in Prague, he studied law at the German University there and worked in a law office to support himself while he wrote in his spare time.

His tyrannical father influenced his literary heroes, who are constantly searching for identity although the nature of this identity is never fully revealed. His literary artistry is full of surprises and shifts, as in his most famous book, *Metamorphosis*. Kafka published some work during his lifetime, but his major works—*The Trial, The Castle,* and *Amerika*—were published only after his death from tuberculosis. Kafka had given his manuscripts to his friend Max Brod and ordered them to be destroyed after his death, but Brod, understanding the importance of those literary works, decided to publish them. Brod later became Kafka's biographer.

Kafka's work has been translated into many languages and helped form the basis for the so-called Theater of the Absurd. *Kafkaesque* became an international expression to describe the feeling of being trapped in a maze of grotesque happenings.

Like most assimilated Jews from Prague, Kafka became aware of his Jewish heritage only in the latter part of his life. From Max Brod he heard about Zionism, while other Jewish friends spoke to him of various Jewish trends. Kafka started studying Hebrew and Judaism, and after he met Dora Dymant he even toyed with the idea of settling in Palestine, an idea that he never acted on.

ISAAC BASHEVIS SINGER *(1904–1991)*

Isaac Bashevis Singer, a Yiddish-writing Nobel Prize–winning novelist, was born into a rabbinical family in Poland that immigrated to America in 1935. He received a traditional education at a seminary that also taught secular studies.

Brought up in a poor village, he steeped himself in the Jewish mysticism of the Kabbalah, a world that he vividly describes in his work. His literary merit was recognized early in his career, and his helpless heroes, trapped within their passions, became famous all over the world.

In 1950 his stories began to appear in translation in serious magazines, and his marvelous tales, filled with demons, imps, and spirits engaged in the complexities of human behavior, caught the attention of believing audiences. Many of his stories were adapted for the stage, and such film productions as *Yentl, The Magician of Lublin,* and *Enemies* brought his spiritual tales to a vast number of viewers worldwide.

Yom Kippur

The Lord spoke to Moses saying:
"Howbeit on the tenth day of this
seventh month is the Day of Atonement: It shall be a holy convocation to you, and you shall
afflict your souls . . . you shall do no manner of work in that same day; for it is a Day of Atone-
ment, to make atonement for you before the Lord your God." (Leviticus 23:26–28)

The ten days that fall between Rosh Hashanah and Yom Kippur are known as the Ten Days of Penitence, solemn days for every Jew. Each soul awaits judgment. The night before Yom Kippur, the ritual of *kaparot* is performed in some traditional communities. A rooster or hen or money in a handkerchief is swung in a circle above the heads of those present nine times, while the person conducting the ceremony recites: "This is instead of me, this is an offering on my account, this is in expiation for me; this rooster shall go to his death, and may I enter a long and healthy life." The rooster is then slaughtered by the shochet and traditionally given to the poor. Because of its closeness to paganism and magic, the ritual has attracted opposition, particularly among rabbis.

Yom Kippur, the Day of Atonement, is a holiday when Jews pray and ask God for forgiveness.

This drawing illustrates a Yom Kippur service on the battlefield at Antwerp in 1914.

Before sundown, Jews eat a special meal, which precedes the strictest fast of the year. People have made their wishes for the new year, performed all the required tasks, and requested forgiveness. It is now time for the Almighty to make His judgment: Yom Hakippurim.

Synagogues are crowded. Many Jews who do not attend temple services all year long come for Yom Kippur, the Day of Atonement. Many men and women dress in white and wear non-leather shoes. The cantor starts singing the haunting opening prayer, Kol Nidrei, which states that all vows made and not fulfilled during the previous (in some formulations, the coming) year are canceled. For the next twenty-four hours, the Jewish people consider their faults and pray for forgiveness and a good judgment.

Many North African Jews stand on hard chick-peas throughout the Yom Kippur prayers in order to remind themselves of their corporeal and mortal fragility. During the day, children may sniff a quince that was immersed in a flower paste for a few days; it is said to lessen the hunger pangs brought on by fasting. Adults often inhale the smell of tobacco dipped in perfume.

On the following day at sundown, the service of Neilah, the closing of the heavenly gates, concludes Yom Kippur. The verdict has been given. When three stars are seen shining in the sky, one long blast of the shofar announces the end of Yom Kippur.

Sukkot

סוכות

*On the fifteenth day of this seventh month is the Feast
of Tabernacles for seven days unto the Lord. On the first
day shall be a holy convocation; you shall do no manner of servile work . . . on the eighth
day shall be a holy convocation unto you . . . it is the day of solemn assembly.*
(Leviticus 23:34–36)

On the day after Yom Kippur, Jews start building their *sukkah*, temporary huts roofed with greens and decorated with fruits of the harvest. Jews are obliged to take their meals and relax in the sukkah for seven days. Historically, the custom recalls the time when the Children of Israel wandered in the desert for forty years and lived in huts. A more spiritual interpretation emphasizes Jews' trust in God's protection: Though sitting in a temporary shelter, the people of Israel trust the Lord to provide them with all their needs, worship Him, and love His ways. Sukkot is also one of three holidays—along with Pesach and Shavuot—during which ancient Jews used to make a pilgrimage to the Temple in Jerusalem.

Sukkot is a happy time of the year. Referred to as the Feast of Tabernacles, the Festival of Booths, and the Festival of the Ingathering, it is the Jewish autumn festival, when people reap the results of their work in the field. A period of joy, in the prayer book it is called "the time of our rejoicing," *Z'man Simchateinu.*

The sukkah, *a temporary hut, is covered with beautiful
ornaments and handmade decorations. This decoration was made
by David Luzzatto in 1833.*

Building the sukkah is great fun for the family. The sukkah must have at least three temporary walls; the fourth "wall" can be open. The roof, *sechach*, must also be temporary and is usually made of tree branches; one must be able to see the stars at night through the branches. Children take great pride in decorating their sukkah. Besides fruit, they often use vegetables, nuts, flowers, paper ornaments, and colorful lights. Families should spend as much time as possible in the sukkah. Even in cold areas, meals should be eaten in the sukkah if possible.

Tunisian Jews made the walls of their sukkah from palm leaves and the doors from arched myrtle branches. The opening had to be shorter than the average adult; this forced all who entered to bend and bow. In Morocco, the hut was made of palm leaves or reeds. Moroccan Jews used to hang a stool on one of the walls for Elijah the prophet. The stool, wrapped in beautiful fabrics, served as a shelf for all the prayer books needed for the holiday. One Sukkot custom honors symbolic guests, *ushpizin*, who are invited to sit in the sukkah. Each day another hero—among them are Abraham, Moses, David, and Joseph—is invited to join the real guests.

The following commandment forms the basis of a beautiful ritual: "And you shall take you on the first day the fruit of goodly trees, branches of palm trees, and boughs of thick trees, and willows of the brook, and you shall rejoice before the Lord your God seven days" (Leviticus 23:40). From these words comes the blessing of the four species: the *etrog* (a citron), *lulav* (a palm branch), *hadas* (a myrtle branch), and *aravah* (a willow branch). Holding the lulav, hadas, and aravah tied together in the right hand and the etrog with its tip down in the left hand, then bringing the two hands together, one recites: "Blessed art Thou, Lord our King of the universe, Who has sanctified us with His commandments and commanded us concerning the taking of the lulav." One then turns the etrog tip up and shakes the lulav.

Interpretations abound. Some view the ritual as a talisman for rain, others believe that the four species symbolize four types of Jews—those with education and good deeds, those without either, and those with one or the other.

81

This sukkah *decoration from Montreal tells about the tradition of inviting the* ushpizin, *guests, into the* sukkah.

82

"And you shall take you on the first day the fruit of goodly trees, branches of palm trees, and boughs of thick trees, and willows of the brook."

Every day of Sukkot, the community gathers in the synagogue for the ritual of *Hoshana*. This is in commemoration of the same ritual performed in the Temple, a talisman for making the earth fertile. On the seventh day, known also as *Hoshana Rabah*, seven such processions are performed.

The last day of Sukkot in Israel is the most joyfully celebrated festival of the Jewish calendar—*Shemini Atzeret* and *Simchat Torah*. Jews leave the sukkah and go back to using their permanent house. Outside of Israel, they are celebrated on separate days.

In celebration of Simchat Torah, the yearly cycle of reading the Torah is completed, and a new cycle starts the following day.

The synagogue is well lit. *Simchat Torah* means, roughly, "*joy* of the Torah," so children participate in high spirits, carrying specially decorated flags, sometimes with an apple on their sticks. The Torah is taken out of the ark and the congregation anticipates the *hakafot*, or circuits. The leader or other members of the synagogue take turns holding the Torah and circling the synagogue, dancing and singing spirited religious and liturgical songs for hours and hours. As the Torah passes, people kiss a scarf or cloth and touch the Torah with it as a sign of respect. The most well-known Simchat Torah celebrations are conducted by the Western Wall in Jerusalem. Seeing that is, for many Jews, witnessing religious ecstasy at its peak.

83

This sukkah decoration from Italy was made in 1813.

IRVING BERLIN *(1888–1990)*

The son of a cantor, Irving Berlin was born Israel Baline in Russia. After coming to New York in 1893, he wrote his first song while working as a singing waiter at a restaurant. Berlin wrote more than one thousand lovable, popular songs despite not having had any formal musical training. His first great success came in 1912, when he wrote "Alexander's Ragtime Band." But his best-loved songs, which put him in the American Hall of Fame of songwriters, include "White Christmas" and "God Bless America," which won him a special gold medal from President Eisenhower. Berlin also wrote the music for such Broadway shows as *Annie Get Your Gun* and *Call Me Madam*, as well as many film scores. He was—and still is in spirit—one of the most popular songwriters in the United States.

SAUL BELLOW *(1915–)*

Saul Bellow, the son of a Russian immigrant, was born in Canada and grew up in both Montreal and Chicago. This multitalented novelist, who received the Nobel Prize for Literature in 1976, had a trilingual childhood. He spoke Yiddish, French, and English. His first novel, *Dangling Man*, was published in 1944. Twenty years later, he became an internationally best-selling author with his most widely acclaimed work, *Herzog*. It is the story of a Jewish professor who struggles comically yet unsuccessfully to relate to a dehumanized world in a human way. *Herzog* placed Bellow among the leading North American novelists. Since then he has written a wealth of books, among them *The Dean's December*; *Henderson, The Rain King*; and *To Jerusalem and Back*.

LEONARD BERNSTEIN *(1918–1990)*

Leonard Bernstein was one of the most intelligent, enthusiastic, and loved composers and conductors of the twentieth century. Born in Massachusetts, he studied composition at Harvard and soon after joined Serge Koussevitzky's conducting class at Tanglewood, a music retreat in Lenox, Massachusetts.

Bernstein attracted national attention after being appointed Assistant Conductor of the New York Philharmonic at the age of twenty-five. When called upon to conduct a difficult program on short notice, he did it brilliantly.

In 1958 he was promoted to music director and conductor of the New York Philharmonic, thus becoming the first American-born musician to occupy this position. In 1969, he went into semiretirement to compose.

Bernstein was not only a great conductor but also a phenomenal composer. He wrote world-acclaimed symphonies such as the *Jeremiah Symphony* (to a biblical text) and the moving *Kaddish*, an oratorio for narrator, chorus, and orchestra, which he conducted for the first time in Tel Aviv. But his most beloved work, *West Side Story*, touched the hearts of the nation. His other musicals are considered classics, too: *On the Town, Wonderful Town,* and *Candide*. Bernstein was closely associated with Israeli musical life and appeared numerous times with various Israeli orchestras.

JEROME ROBBINS *(1918–1991)*

Jerome Robbins was born Jerome Rabinowitz in New York City. Director, choreographer, and producer, he put a unique stamp on ballet and musical theater in the United States. He joined the Ballet Theater in 1940, where he danced his first important role two years later, conveying expressive interpretations of comic and dramatic characters.

His first choreographed piece, *Fancy Free*, was based on contemporary movement and became such a great success that it was expanded into the hit musical *On the Town*. In 1948, he became the associate artistic director of the New York City Ballet. For many people, his most noted achievement was the raw, energized choreography of *West Side Story*, which he choreographed both on Broadway and for the motion picture.

For a few years, Robbins operated his own successful dance company, after which he went on to choreograph another hit, *Fiddler on the Roof*. Many of his creations are still being performed throughout the world. He was also an enthusiastic supporter of the Israeli-Yemenite Inbal dance company.

This nineteenth-century Simchat Torah flag is a woodcut from Poland.

85

Children hold flags such as this one
while dancing and rejoicing during the
Simchat Torah celebrations.

POSTBIBLICAL HOLIDAYS

Chanukah

חנוכה

The two months between Sukkot and Chanukah are long. Weather in temperate climates in the Northern Hemisphere is usually cloudy and rainy. And then comes Chanukah. A most popular festival among children, it is a joyful eight days filled with songs, games, and presents.

Chanukah, a postbiblical festival, is not sanctified with a Sabbathlike atmosphere. On the twenty-fifth day of the Jewish month of Kislev, which falls in December, the historic victory of the Maccabees is commemorated. The Jews, led by Judah Maccabee, struggled against the Syrian-Greek regime that tried to impose restrictions on the practice of Judaism. *Chanukah* means "dedication" and celebrates the rededication of the Temple to the service of God after its defilement by pagans.

This eighteenth-century hanukiya, *a Chanukah menorah, is from Frankfurt.*

Chanukah also goes by the name of the Festival of Lights. Every day at nightfall, the family gathers around the *menorah*, a candelabra with eight branches and an additional branch for the service light, the *shamash*. The family lights the candles with the shamash and recites the blessing: "Blessed art Thou, Lord our God, King of the universe, Who has sanctified us with His commandments and commanded us to kindle the Chanukah light. Blessed art Thou, Lord our God, King of the universe, Who performed miracles for our forefathers in those days, at this time." Each day another candle is added in sequence, until all eight candles are lit on the eighth day. It is a good deed to watch the candles burn, and many people place the menorah in a window so that passersby may see the lights.

This silver hanukiya *was made by the firm of Alexander Sturm in Vienna circa 1900.*

The tradition of lighting the menorah is based on a colorful story, which took place in 165 B.C.E. (Before the Common Era) during the time of the Maccabees, the family who won the fight with the Syrian Greeks. When the Maccabees came back to the Temple, they found that there was only one small flask of oil left to light the menorah. But a miracle occurred, and the tiny amount of oil lasted for eight days.

Traditional foods served on Chanukah include dairy dishes and potato pancakes (*latkes*). But the best of all are *sufganiot*, doughnuts filled with delicious jelly. The spinning of the dreidel also became symbolic of this holiday. The dreidel is a four-sided top with the Hebrew letters *nun*, *gimel*, *hei*, and *shin* shown on each side. The letters stand for Hebrew words that mean "A great miracle happened there."

Chanukah also commemorates Judith's miracle. A beautiful and righteous widow who decided to thwart the Greeks' plot to conquer her village, she managed to enter the tent of the army's highest officer and seduce him. During dinner, she slipped him a sleeping potion; once he fell asleep, she killed him, cut off his head, and put it into a sack. When stopped by his officers, she opened the sack only to see some red grapes—a miracle had occurred. When the Greeks found out that their leader was dead, they fled.

In Tunisia, this story became the basis for the "Holiday of Girls," in which the woman of the house baked honey cakes and sent them to all the single girls in the village, while all the affianced young men sent presents to their fiancées and celebrated their engagements with a great feast.

Purim

Once, in the land of Persia, there lived the great King Ahasuerus, who ruled over the land with his queen, Vashti. One day, wanting to show off his greatness and wealth, he decided to throw a feast. On the seventh day of the festival, the king, after having too much to drink, called for his queen to appear and show off her beauty to his officials. The queen refused and was banished.

Wanting a new wife, the king held a contest among all the eligible women in his kingdom. He chose a beautiful Jewish girl, Esther, who had been raised by her uncle, Mordechai, to be queen. Years later, the king's evil advisor, Haman, commanded all people to show their respect to him by bowing. All but Mordechai obliged. Wanting to punish him, Haman plotted to destroy the entire Jewish population by convincing the foolish king to kill all the Jews in his kingdom.

88

Mordechai the Jew, who raised his niece Esther to be a queen.

This diorama, which depicts Esther coming to King Ahasuerus, is by an unknown artist of the early nineteenth century.

Mordechai, upon hearing the news, went into mourning, wore sackcloth, and begged Esther to plead for her people. Esther asked him to fast for three days, after which she would go to the king. Esther invited the king and Haman to a banquet. While they ate, she invited them to yet another one, to take place on the following evening. Haman, filled with pride for being invited to such important events, left that night content. On his way home, he spotted Mordechai wandering in the palace and that enraged him. At his wife's advice, Haman plotted to have Mordechai hung from a tall tree.

That night Ahasuerus couldn't fall asleep. He asked two of his servants to read to him from his Book of Chronicles. He discovered that Mordechai had never been rewarded for saving him from an assassination plot. At that moment, Haman walked in to ask the king's permission to hang Mordechai. Instead, the king asked Haman's advice with respect to Mordechai's reward. He asked Haman: "What should be done to a man the king wishes to reward?" Haman, thinking he was the one to be rewarded, replied that the man should be dressed in royal clothing, paraded on a royal horse through the streets of Shushan, the capital, and led by an official who would announce: "This is what is done to the man the king wishes to honor." The king ordered Haman to carry out his suggestion—for Mordechai!

90

These Purim masks of Queen Esther, King Ahasuerus, and wicked Haman were created by Mimi Gross.

After walking Mordechai through the streets of the city, Haman came to Esther's second banquet, where she revealed his plot to destroy the Jews. Enraged, the king ordered Haman hung on the same tree he had prepared for Mordechai. He then picked Mordechai to be his advisor. The shifting of fortune, as told in the story of Esther, has provided great hope to Jews throughout the centuries.

The word *Purim* comes from the word *pur*, for "lottery," the method used by Haman to select a day for destroying the Jews. On the fourteenth day of Adar, Purim is celebrated by Jews all over the world. On Purim eve, the congregation gathers in the synagogue to listen to the reading of the Scroll of Esther, the *Megillah*. Children wear costumes and yell and rattle noisemakers each time they hear the name of the terrible Haman in the *Megillah*.

Jews are commanded to eat, drink, and be merry on this happy festival. Most Jewish communities hold great carnival-like celebrations and costume parades. In Tel Aviv, a famous Purim parade, which ceased to exist for ten years, was reintroduced in 1980 and is the highlight of an Israeli's Purim.

The day before Purim is the Fast of Esther. Young Tunisian girls used to cut a curl from their hair, throw it into a well, and ask Esther to give them some of her beauty. On the Sabbath before the festival, children would parade around the Jewish quarters, holding onto a big ugly doll symbolizing Haman and proclaiming his meanness. At the end of the parade, they burned this doll. Needy children knocked on people's doors to ask for money.

The oldest custom of Purim is *mishloach manot*, the sending of food, especially sweets, to friends and to the poor. Fruits, various baked goods, wine, and other goodies are delivered in baskets or on plates. A specially baked triangle cookie filled with poppy seeds or prunes, called *hamantaschen*, is the official pastry of this holiday. Many people also send gifts of money to needy families on Purim.

91

This Purim masquerade is from Sefer Minhagim *(the Book of Customs, Venice, 1593).*

Tu Bishvat

The fifteenth day of the Jewish month of Shevat is mentioned by the Mishna as the beginning of the "New Year for the Trees." This holiday has become a sort of Jewish Arbor Day, when Jews plant trees and eat dried fruits. Being an agricultural community, Israel celebrates this less religious and more secular, nature-oriented holiday more enthusiastically than the rest of the Jewish world. Each child brings dried fruits to school, and usually around noon, everyone goes out to plant new trees in their local forest. It is a common sight to see an Israeli child returning home on that day, holding a little tree or plant that he will plant in a home garden.

Some Jews in North America and Israel have revived the custom, originated by sixteenth-century kabbalists (Jewish mystics) and continued by Sephardim, of a Tu Bishvat seder, modeled after the Passover seder and incorporating different kinds of fruit, four cups of wine, and readings and songs (from the Torah, modern Israel, and elsewhere) about trees.

This table is set for Tu Bishvat, the celebration of the "New Year for the Trees."

Lag Baomer

This merry holiday, celebrated on the thirty-third day between Passover and Shavuot, is mentioned in connection with the festival of Shavuot. It is said that on this day the plague that killed many of Rabbi Akiva's disciples (and made the days of the omer a semi-mourning period) ended. This is the day within the counting of the omer when weddings and other *simchot* (happy celebrations) can take place.

In Israel, children go out to forests with archers' bows. When night falls, celebrants light bonfires across the country. The seashore looks especially dramatic. Songs are sung all over to the accompaniment of an accordion or a guitar; the party lasts into the wee hours of the night. It is the custom to roast potatoes in the bonfires, and most children return home smudged with black marks from the charred potatoes.

Lag Baomer is also the time when the kabbalists commemorate their famous father of mysticism, Rabbi Shimon bar Yochai. The revelry that takes place at his gravesite in Meiron attracts thousands of people annually. Many pious followers bring their three-year-old boys to get their first haircut there and to receive the blessing of his spirit. Day and night, people from all over the country gather around the site, to pray, sing, dance, cook out, and light candles, believing this ritual to portend a fruitful and happy life.

92

This brass and cloisonné omer calendar is from Italy.

93

Tisha Be'av

On the ninth day of the Jewish month of Av, Jews fast and mourn the destruction of the Temple (twice) in Jerusalem and the resultant exiles of the Jews from their homeland. The destruction of the Temple has remained, for traditional Jews, the ultimate symbol of great Jewish tragedy.

Tisha Be'av marks the end of three weeks of semi-mourning that starts with the fast of the Seventeenth of Tamuz (the first day the walls of Jerusalem were breached by attacking Babylonians). During these three weeks, all signs of happiness disappear from traditional Jewish communities; all celebrations are forbidden. People may cut their hair or shave, but during the last nine days before Tisha Be'av, no one may bathe or eat meat.

The last day is a day of fasting, like Yom Kippur. Mourners wear rubber shoes (as leather ones are, as on Yom Kippur, not allowed), sit on low stools in the synagogue reading chapters from the Book of Lamentations (*Eichah*), and sing dirges (*kinot*). In a mournful key, they remember for a whole evening the great disaster of so many years ago that set the course of Jewish history for centuries.

Yom Hashoah
(Holocaust Memorial Day)

Since the European Holocaust of World War II, another memorial day has joined those already commemorating the long history of the Jewish people. Six million Jews (and countless others) were killed by the Nazi war machine headed by Adolf Hitler. Six million Jews were burned, choked, shot, gassed, or annihilated in ways no ethical mind can grasp. This criminal show of racism at its worst has affected the entire human race. No special religious rituals are attached to the twenty-seventh day of the Jewish month of Nisan, which is the official memorial day for Jews murdered in the Holocaust. Throughout the world, however, Jews and non-Jews alike conduct ceremonies to remember those who were slaughtered.

On that day in Israel a unique atmosphere permeates the country. It has no comparison to any other holiday or celebration, religious or secular, held during the year. The entire nation, a haven for many who lost loved ones to Hitler's insane Final Solution, pauses for two minutes when a siren blows. Cars stop on the roads, and people cease their tasks.

In Yad Vashem, the official memorial shrine where an eternal flame burns, a ceremony is conducted. Every town and every village holds a ceremony. Radio and television stations broadcast special programs and movies related to this horrible event. Israel bows its head to those people who contributed directly to the survival of the Jewish people and to the birth of the State of Israel.

94

This drawing was done by a child in a Nazi concentration camp.

ANNE FRANK *(1929–1945)*

The diary of fourteen-year-old Anne Frank has captivated the hearts of readers all over the world. Anne Frank was born in Germany and fled to Amsterdam after the Nazis rose to power. When the deportation of Jews from Holland began, her family went into hiding in the back of the Franks' business offices. They stayed there for two years, until they were betrayed and turned over to the Germans.

Anne Frank wrote her diary during her years in hiding. She described in a clear and articulate voice her life during those turbulent years during the Holocaust. She depicted life under Nazi terror with an unusually mature literary perception and great psychological insight. The diary was found after her death in the Bergen-Belsen concentration camp and has been translated into more than forty languages. Anne Frank's hiding place in Amsterdam has since been turned into a museum.

All Jews were forced by the Nazis to wear a patch in the shape of a Jewish star to mark their identities.

95

Yom Ha'atzmaut (Israeli Independence Day)

יום העצמאות

The fifth day of the Jewish month of Iyar commemorates a new era in Jewish life, the birth of the State of Israel. Two thousand years after their exile, Jews from all over the world returned to their homeland to build themselves a haven, to rebuild a formal nation. The United Nations voted in one historic moment to grant the Jewish people a fulfillment of their forefathers' dreams—a land of their own. Since then, a new date, Yom Ha'atzmaut, was added to the Jewish calendar.

Communities around the world celebrate this day with prayers in synagogues and festivals of dances and songs. In Israel, the day is combined with the remembrance of the price Jews have had to pay in order to achieve, and secure, Israeli independence. The day before Independence Day, Israelis mourn their loved ones who died during their various wars. This is a sad day in this old-new country. Every Israeli citizen knows of at least one close friend or relative who lost his life protecting the country. Memorial services in army graveyards are often punctuated by mourners' cries.

Paradoxically, only a siren blast separates the sadness of memorial services from the happiness of celebrating Independence Day. At seven o'clock in the evening, the wail of the siren sounds throughout the country. People stand still for a final commemorative moment and then officially begin the celebrations. As usual in Jewish life, sadness and happiness are intermingled.

Fireworks are launched, accompanied by performances and parades. The celebrations continue until early the next morning. The following day everyone has off from work or school, and people spend it picnicking or enjoying intimate get-togethers.

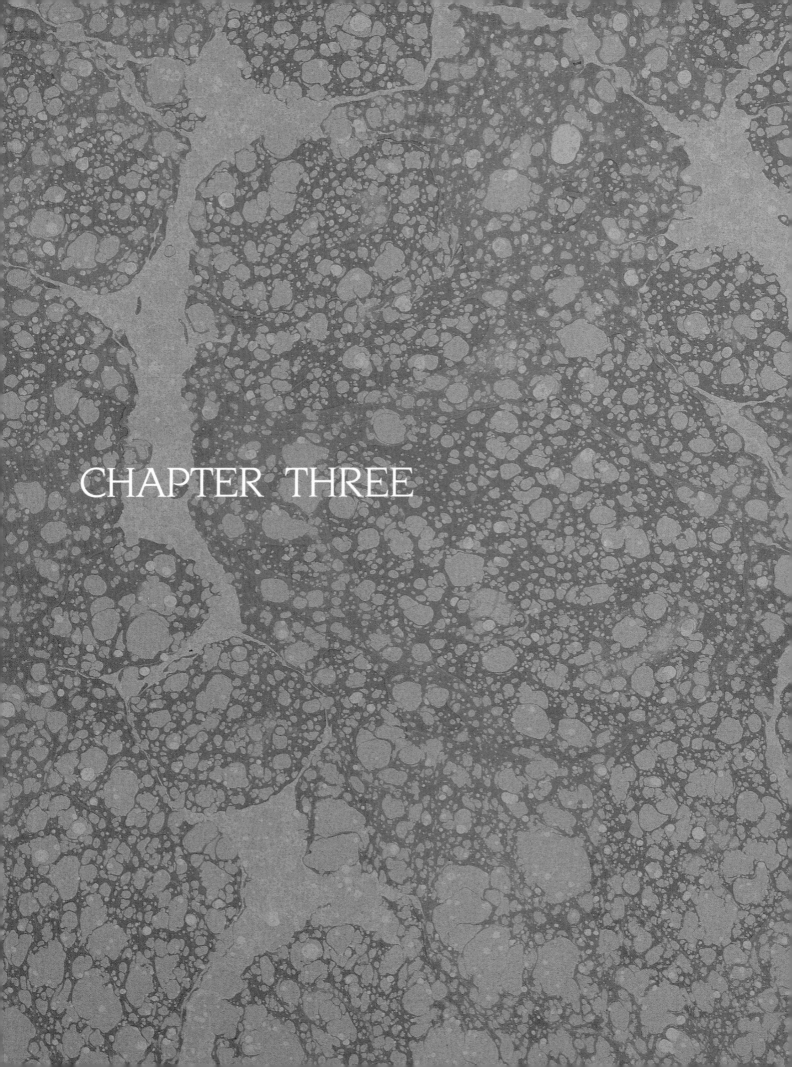

CHAPTER THREE

WORLD JEWRY

The year 70 of the common era was a turning point in Jewish history. The Roman army, headed by Titus the Emperor, attacked Jerusalem and destroyed the Second Temple. The independent State of Judea ceased to exist, and Jews were forced to leave their homeland. The end of Jewish statehood marked the beginning of the dispersion of the Jewish people all across the globe into what became known as the Diaspora, or the *Golah*. The scattered Jewish communities of the world, although greatly contributing to the local economies, culture, and political life, became targets of anti-Semitism and discrimination.

When pushed out of one country or persecuted in another, Jews moved on to a new territory. Whenever a migration center showed signs of danger, communities would pick up and settle somewhere safer. While clinging to their faith and customs of worship, Jews managed to adapt to a succession of environments, continents, languages, and occupations.

When expelled from Spain at the height of the Inquisition, Jews found refuge in North Africa, Italy, and the Ottoman Empire. After suffering persecution in medieval Germany, they traveled east to Poland and Lithuania. And to escape the oppression of life in nineteenth-century Russia, hundreds of thousands of Jews crossed oceans to the United States, Canada, Latin America, South Africa, and Australia.

Despite widespread and unrelenting persecution, Jews have managed to preserve their religion, heritage, and ancient traditions. These traditions, performed in accordance with the laws of Moses and the rabbis, have sustained the Jewish people throughout centuries of turbulent existence.

The birth of the State of Israel in 1948 began a new era for Jewish life in the Diaspora. The existence of a homeland and a safe refuge has provided security and hope for Jewish souls all over the world.

The identity of the Jewish people in the Diaspora has been kept alive through the workings of one very important institution: the synagogue. In most Jewish communities the world over, the synagogue serves not only as a place of worship but also as the center of Jewish life. The rabbi, who heads the synagogue, is considered the head of the community and helps to solve community matters. In the United States, several governing committees are also maintained to oversee other extensions of the synagogue, such as Hebrew schools and youth organizations. Every major Jewish community in the Diaspora also maintains charitable and communal service organizations, without which the Diaspora could not have survived throughout the years.

These basic structures, however varied in form, have been part and parcel of the Jewish world in the Diaspora for centuries. When a Jew was forced to move from one place to another, the structure of the new community would always be familiar to him and as a result would ease his eventual absorption.

RUSSIAN JEWS

In the past, Jewish people lived in large communities all over Eastern Europe. The heroic story of the distinguished Polish community is still in the process of being recorded and reconstructed by survivors of the Holocaust. Romanian, Yugoslavian, Hungarian, and other Jewish communities have virtually disappeared. One of the most fascinating stories, however, has unfolded behind what was once the Iron Curtain: the story of Soviet Jewry.

Writing the history of Soviet Jewry is still a difficult if not impossible task, however, owing to the dramatic upheaval still taking place in the former Soviet Union and Eastern Bloc countries. A hundred years ago, Russia was host to the world's largest Jewish community, which at its peak numbered more than five million: a vibrant and vigorous community, which managed to maintain its identity despite tides of anti-Semitism. As of 1990, the Soviet Union still hosted the third-largest Jewish community in the world, after the United States and Israel. The figures are changing, however, as thousands of Jews leave this region to find new homes in Israel and the West in a migration that could rival the exodus of Russian Jews at the turn of the century.

Russian Jews contributed, when allowed, to the literature, economy, science, technology, arts, and industry of their adopted homeland. For their achievements,

This 1882 engraving depicts Jews being expelled from the town of Podosk in Russia.

they were both praised and persecuted, hated and applauded. The turmoil of the 1917 revolution left Russian Jewry confused and divided: they had to choose between embracing the newly established revolutionary culture or leaving the country. Many who could not stand the tension assimilated and were lost inside the vast country. Others chose to secretly deepen their Jewish identity.

Russian Jewry's search for individual and collective solutions played an important role in the development of modern world Jewry. The large migration of Russian Jews to America at the turn of the twentieth century dramatically influenced the shape and character of American Jewry. Russian Jews also played a key role in forming the Zionist movement and in creating the new settlement in Palestine that in 1948 became the State of Israel. Today, history is repeating itself with a twist as Russian Jews again play a key role in Israel's development. Hundreds of thousands of Jews have emigrated in the past few years, with perhaps a million expected to join them in the next decade.

The history of Russian Jewry has always been turbulent. The czars tried to keep Jews completely out of their territories; in 1727, all Jews were formally expelled from Russia, and in 1739, they were ordered to leave the territories annexed by Russia, the Ukraine, and Byelorussia. Even though many Jews made tremendous efforts to become an integral part of Russian society, only in the last hundred years or so did the Jews start to mingle successfully among their Russian neighbors, and they still had to fight prejudice and anti-Semitism.

Against tremendous odds of oppression and official intolerance, Jewish culture prospered in nineteenth-century Russia. Unable to depend on government help,

100

Until the 1917 Russian Revolution, young men received their education in the cheder, *an all-in-one classroom for Hebrew studies.*

MARC CHAGALL *(1887–1985)*

Marc Chagall, born Marc Segal in Russia, was a member of the Surrealist Movement. He studied art in Leningrad and moved to Paris at the age of twenty-three. Although he lived most of his life in France, Chagall's paintings captured life in his childhood village in Russia. Many are based on Jewish ghetto themes, portraying life in the *shtetl*.

In 1914, Chagall returned to Russia to serve as the government's Commissar of Arts. He was also appointed designer for the Chamber State Jewish Theater in Moscow. Chagall's works, which were influenced by the Cubist style of Picasso and Braque, later shocked the Communist party, and he left to go back to France.

After returning to France in 1923, Chagall gained great fame and was considered a leading figure in the artistic world. In 1941, fearing Nazi conquest, Chagall fled France for New York, but he returned to Paris in 1948, where he lived for the rest of his life.

Marc Chagall's works are featured in museum collections throughout the world. His famous stained-glass windows catch the light at such acclaimed sites as the Hadassah Medical Center in Jerusalem and the Metropolitan Opera House in New York City.

Russian Jews developed an impressive chain of institutions and establishments that were dedicated to preserving their heritage and culture. Many of these communal institutions performed the tasks of a modern welfare state. Until the late nineteenth century, authorities acknowledged the local Jewish communal bodies (*kahals*), which were in charge of health, education, and welfare in the Jewish community. Even after the czar's official abolishment of these institutions, the communities continued to run their own affairs as before, while establishing new institutions—hospitals, orphanages, old-age homes—for helping the needy.

A unique feature of the Jewish community was the *cheder*, a kind of all-in-one classroom for Hebrew studies, which was the dominant form of education until the 1917 revolution. Each cheder was conducted by a teacher, a *melamed*, who taught the boys of the community from the age of three up until the time of their bar mitzvah. (After that, they attended a yeshiva.) Surprisingly, to be a melamed was looked down upon; the community considered him an unsuccessful person. Very few girls received any formal Jewish education.

The turn of the century brought with it changes in Jewish education that coincided with the tides of change running through Russian politics. Many new schools were formed that leaned toward socialism and were taught in both Hebrew and Yiddish. Up until then, Hebrew was used only in the teaching of Judaic studies, as it was considered a holy language. The beginning of the twentieth century, however, introduced the use of Hebrew in all aspects of life. Gifted writers began to express themselves in both Hebrew and Yiddish, which gave birth to a fresh body of literature that included the works of Micha Yosef Berdichevsky and Chaim Nachman Bialik, whose poems reflect his great admiration and appreciation of the world of study and Judaism. Ahad Haam became a famous essayist, whose clear, crisp compositions contributed to the rise of the Zionist idea. Two classical Yiddish writers, Shalom Aleichem and I.L. Peretz, enriched Jewish literature with their stories and to this day are still considered cornerstones of Jewish cultural heritage. Shalom Aleichem is probably the best-known Jewish writer; *Fiddler on the Roof* was based on one of his stories, and his works have been translated all over the world. Even though his writings deal exclusively with the lives of turn-of-the-century Russian Jewry, his themes are universal and have an international appeal.

Although most Jews greeted the 1917 revolution enthusiastically, they quickly discovered that many disparate groups in the war-torn country used them as scapegoats. The freedom won by Jews in the short period leading up to the

101

ARTHUR RUBENSTEIN *(1886–1990)*

Piano virtuoso Arthur Rubenstein started his career in Poland at the age of three. He played his first international concert to a cheering crowd at the age of eleven, with the Berlin Symphony.

In 1937, he made the United States his home, and from there he traveled all over the world, playing with the greatest orchestras. Rubenstein also composed piano and chamber music. Maestro Rubenstein may be most loved, however, for his dedication as an educator who taught and advised young musicians around the globe. The Rubenstein Piano Competition, which takes place in Israel, is a great challenge to young pianists from every country. Winning this prestigious musical event opens the doors of the professional music world to brilliant new pianists every year.

revolution quickly evaporated into a renewed and more terrible wave of restrictive anti-Semitism, including vicious pogroms mounted by armed groups.

The new Communist party considered Jewish values and communal institutions to be alien to Marxist ideology. As a result, the party was determined to end all religious and Zionist activities. In the years following the revolution, thousands of Zionists were arrested and exiled to Siberia. The remainder of the Zionist movement and the Jewish cultural communities were forced underground. All Hebrew culture was banned, and in reaction, writers and poets such as Bialik, Saul Tsh'rnichovksy, and B.Z. Ginzburg left Russia—as did the acclaimed Habimah theater group, which didn't return home after a tour abroad.

The new Communist government came out in force against all religions, including Judaism. Synagogues were ordered closed, and in many cases, Jews were killed defending their houses of worship. Jews also had to give up celebrating holidays and the Sabbath, which were considered working days for the general public, and penalties for not showing up for work were very high. As Yiddish was still a legal language, many Yiddish-speaking schools appeared in the 1920s. These schools were Jewish only in language; they served the Communist state and were forbidden to teach Jewish subjects. Also, most of these Yiddish schools taught only through the elementary level; parents who wanted their children to get a higher education had to send them to Russian schools. In short order, most of the Jewish community resisted the Yiddish schools, feeling that they blocked their children's— and their own—paths of entry into the Soviet world. In little more than a decade, it became very difficult to be an observant Jew in the Soviet Union.

World War II brought the terror of the Holocaust to the Jews in the German-occupied territories of the Soviet Union. Thousands of Soviet Jews were murdered. The most infamous site was the city of Babi Yar, where over thirty thousand Jews were massacred within two days. The Soviet poet Yevgeny Yevtushenko wrote a poem about the killing that caused great controversy in the Soviet Union, as the government did not want to admit that only Jews, because they were Jews, were killed there. The Soviet party line claimed that the non-Jewish population did its best to help Jews minimize their suffering, but survivors have told stories about the native Russian population helping German troops kill their Jewish neighbors.

The years following World War II were dark years for Jewish culture in the Soviet Union. The last Yiddish publication in the country was closed, and several hundred Jewish activists were arrested and exiled. The anti-cosmopolitan campaign that forbade Western culture from entering Soviet borders made the Jews pay the price. In Stalin's day, many qualified Jews were fired and refused jobs. Jews were not accepted into schools and universities. Surprisingly though, at the same time the Soviet government was restricting its own Jewish population, it enthusiastically supported the establishment of the State of Israel.

HENRY KISSINGER *(1923–   )*

Born in Germany, Henry Kissinger came to the United States in 1938 and became the most famous political analyst of our time. A Harvard graduate, Kissinger is an expert in defense policy and international relations. He served as an advisor on national security affairs to presidents John F. Kennedy and Richard Nixon and became Secretary of State under Nixon in 1968. As presidential confidant and Nixon's main advisor on security, foreign affairs, and nuclear disarmament, Kissinger helped form international policy for many years.

Kissinger served as a mediator in the Arab-Israeli conflict from 1968 to 1973 and in many other peace negotiations around the world. He is a lecturer and best-selling writer, and in 1973, he received the Nobel Peace Prize.

Stalin's death brought only minor relief for Jews; although not officially persecuted, Soviet Jewry remained under fire. Jewish culture was still practically illegal, and anti-Semitism ebbed and flowed during the years following 1953. After the Six Day War in June 1967, the Soviets ceased diplomatic relations with Israel and closed the doors to further Jewish emigration.

A new breed of freedom fighters emerged—*refuseniks*, who dared to apply (usually unsuccessfully) for exit visas and thereby risked their jobs, their apartments, and in some cases, prison sentences and exile. With them came stories of heroism and daring. One well-known story took place in 1970, when eleven Russian Jews were caught while planning to hijack an aircraft and fly it out of the country. Two of them were subsequently sentenced to death, but an international campaign was launched to save their lives and helped focus world attention on the plight of Soviet Jews. Both men were spared, and their highly publicized trial pushed Soviet authorities to let a small number of Jews emigrate to Israel. In their wake, the refusenik movement was born. Jews and non-Jews all over the world took up the cause of Soviet Jewry, writing letters to the Kremlin, pressuring Western leaders, and participating in protest marches and support rallies. This concerted effort helped win the release of imprisoned refuseniks such as Yosef Mendelevich, Yosef Begun, Ida Nudel, and others. Between 1968 and 1987 nearly 270,000 Jews left the Soviet Union for Israel and other countries. In 1990, in the wake of *perestroika*, the Soviet authorities again reopened the gates for what will surely be the largest Russian Jewish emigration of modern times.

The Soviet Union was and still is home to a large number of non-Ashkenazic Jews. These communities—Georgian, Bukharan, and Mountain Jews—have different religious traditions, customs, and social structures. Families in these Sephardic communities are generally much larger than those of their Ashkenazic brothers, and they maintain a strict patriarchal structure. Throughout the twentieth century, they remained fairly isolated from the changes sweeping the Soviet Union, and as a consequence, they managed to hold onto their religious faith and traditions. The only modern trend they willingly adopted was Zionism, because it dovetailed with their religious belief in a return to the Holy Land. Large numbers of Soviet Sephardic Jews emigrated to Israel in the early 1900s and then again in the 1980s.

The past hundred years have been difficult for Russian Jews. Governments and rulers have come and gone, some more and some less tolerant toward the Jews; yet, historically, the Russian people have treated Jews as unwanted outsiders. The relaxed regulations that permit emigration to Israel, however, have brought together a new community of Jews who have turned their passive identity into an active one. They have proved themselves to be a committed group willing to make personal sacrifices in order to maintain a unified national and religious identity.

103

THE NEW WORLD

In 1492, Queen Isabella and King Ferdinand of Spain signed a decree that expelled all Jews from their country. Five days after the last confessed Jew had left Spain (some say it was only one day), Ferdinand and Isabella's protégé, Christopher Columbus, set sail on his voyage of discovery.

Ironically, the same queen and king who rejected Jews in their own country helped to build the future haven for all people suffering from religious persecution. There is another ironic twist to the story: some historians believe that Christopher Columbus himself was a Jew who had converted to Christianity—a Marrano. According to most histories, however, the first Jew to set foot in the New World was Luis de Torres, Columbus' interpreter, who converted to Christianity just before sailing with Columbus.

The United States

By the beginning of the American Revolution in 1776, twenty-five hundred Jews lived in organized communities along the Atlantic corridor, mostly in Montreal, New York, Newport, Philadelphia, Charleston, and Savannah. These Jews, mainly traders, looked and dressed like any other immigrant of that time, and by the

104

The United States was the "Land of Opportunity" for many Jewish newcomers. This sheet music (above, left) was published on Manhattan's Lower East Side, and this New Year's card (above, right) features images of the Statue of Liberty, boats carrying immigrants, American factories, and steam engines.

DANNY KAYE *(1913–1987)*

Funnyman and entertainer Danny Kaye, son of tailor Jacob Kaminsky, was born and brought up in Brooklyn, New York. His brief and unsuitable career as an insurance agent soon pushed him into the profession where he flourished—show business. Beginning in the "Borscht Belt" of the Catskill Mountains, he later appeared on Broadway with great success in 1939 in *The Straw Hat Revue*.

Kaye's big break in show business came in 1941 when Moss Hart wrote a part for him in the musical *Lady in the Dark* after seeing him perform in a New York nightclub; he was a hit. Kaye then went on to Hollywood and made many wonderful films, such as *The Secret Life of Walter Mitty*, *The Inspector General*, and *Hans Christian Andersen*.

Kaye's unique style, which incorporated mime, song, and irony, made him a legend in his own time. Both children and adults loved him, and he served as ambassador-at-large for the United Nations International Children's Fund.

middle of the nineteenth century, all the restrictions placed upon them because of religious differences were removed.

From 1840 on, the number of Jews in the United States increased when thousands of German Jews made their way to find a new life in the New Country. They brought with them a tradition on which the Reform movement was built. They created a new middle-class community, with banking and merchant families who greatly influenced the American economy. Julius Rosenwald (who developed the Sears mail-order business) and Levi Strauss (of blue jeans fame) were only two of the great Jewish businessmen of that era. By 1881, American Jews numbered approximately three hundred thousand. That year also marked the beginning of the great migration of Eastern European Jews to western shores.

These Jews, from Poland, Russia, Romania, and other Balkan and Slavic countries, brought with them a different kind of Judaism that changed the shape and history of the Diaspora. Many were Orthodox, Yiddish-speaking Jews who had left behind a poor socioeconomic situation and had hopes of improving their circumstances in North America. The United States at that time was experiencing rapid economic growth and welcomed the new immigrants with open arms.

The majority of Eastern European immigrants arrived penniless, having spent their life's savings for the ticket to come over. All they carried with them was their enthusiasm and hopes of starting a fresh new life in the "Golden Medina," the golden land of America that everyone in Europe was talking about. Cultural differences kept them apart from their relatively affluent German brothers, and most had no choice but to settle in slum neighborhoods inside the major cities.

They quickly discovered that religious freedom did not guarantee improved economic conditions. The new immigrants, or "greenhorns," as they were wont to be called, rolled up their sleeves and went to work in the sweatshops that had sprung up around their neighborhoods, such as the Lower East Side of Manhattan. Despite the adverse conditions, these eager, hard-working people managed to create and maintain a rich cultural life. Yiddish theater flourished, and Jewish life was conducted according to old traditions and customs. Unlike their parents, the second generation of this Jewish migration attended public schools, expanded into a variety of businesses, moved out of their parents' ghettos, and entered the mainstream of American life. Driven by tremendous energy and the need to prosper, these greenhorn immigrants and their children made impressive inroads into American political, economic, and artistic life, all in a relatively short span of time. And over the years, the Jewish community in the United States developed three main streams of religious practice: Orthodox, Conservative, and Reform.

105

Orthodox

The term *Orthodox Jews*, coined in the beginning of the nineteenth century, relates to those Jews who still accept that the Torah is God's revealed will. In addition, Orthodoxy sees the Talmud as defining the basic framework of Jewish life.

The orthodoxy conceived inside the Eastern European shtetl and brought to the New World has now practically disappeared from the United States. Still, some Orthodox Jewish communities, particularly those in Brooklyn and Monsey, New York, maintain the older traditions. Jews in these communities speak Yiddish and dress much as their ancestors did in eighteenth-century Poland. Men wear long black coats, beards, and earlocks (*payot*); women wear wigs, cover their bodies with longer dresses, and the like. Unlike this relatively small number of ultra-Orthodox Jews, a Modern or Centrist Orthodox Jew in America dresses, speaks, and behaves like any other American. However different these two practices of Judaism may be on the outside, both are still expressions of Orthodoxy. After the birth of the State of Israel, most Orthodox factions accepted Zionism and supported the country enthusiastically. Two sects—the *Satmars* of Brooklyn and *Neturei Karta* in Jerusalem—still reject the Zionist idea, and other Orthodox groups coexist uneasily with the Jewish state.

Conservative

In the middle of the nineteenth century, the Conservative movement was created in Germany and introduced in the United States, where it spread widely as a halfway stand between strict Orthodoxy and the progressive Reform movement. Led by educator and rabbi Solomon Schechter, it followed the basic traditions of the dietary laws, the Hebrew prayer book, and the observance of the Sabbath. The main idea behind the Conservative movement established Judaism as a living tradition, able to adjust and grow within the context of the times without losing its unique characteristics.

The Conservative movement played a key role in the lives of many children who had just emigrated with their parents from Europe. It allowed them to integrate into American life without letting go of their parents' traditions. Today, it is the largest branch of Judaism in the United States. (All three branches, Orthodox, Reform, and Conservative, are represented by the Synagogue Council of America in matters of interfaith activities on a national level.)

Reform

At the end of the eighteenth century, emancipation and the Enlightenment moved a number of people away from traditional Judaism, especially in Germany. This movement became stronger at the beginning of the nineteenth century. Its purpose: to attract younger and more "forward-thinking" Jews to the synagogue. Liturgy was shortened and translated into German; a choir and an organ were introduced into the service. More fundamentally, Reform Jews rejected the idea that Jews constituted a national entity, claiming instead that they were only Germans of Jewish faith—that Judaism was only a religion, rather than a people and civilization.

Reform Judaism flourished in the fertile ground of the nineteenth-century United States, where most Jews claimed German ancestry. In the beginning, Reform Jews flatly declared themselves to be simply a religious community. The Bible was perceived as an instrument for moral instruction, out of which only the laws that had obvious moral value were binding. All Messianic hope was eliminated, and the movement, emphasizing the here and now, preached world justice and peace among all men.

Hasidic Jews maintain older traditions.

The realities of the twentieth century shattered the Reform movement's positive and hopeful view of the Jewish future, as renewed persecution broke out in both Eastern and Western Europe. In time, the Reform movement adopted a new doctrine, closer to traditional Judaism, with a sympathetic attitude toward the Zionist idea and the revival of the biblical language of Hebrew. Reform Judaism today still emphasizes the ethical teachings of the Torah, the Talmud, and other sacred writings, but gives ritual a greater, though still secondary, importance.

About six million Jews—more than half of the world's Jewish population—live in the United States. The different branches of Judaism run their own schools and institutions, but all of them face the same pressing problems: assimilation, intermarriage, and religious apathy. Despite these difficulties, American Jewry approaches the end of the century with a well-founded sense of confidence. No longer do Jews feel compelled to hide their religion in order to succeed in life. Millions of Jewish immigrants, their children, and their children's children have found in the United States a free, open society where they can express themselves personally and religiously.

Discriminatory practices do still exist, along with such anti-Semitic organizations as the Ku Klux Klan and a handful of neo-Nazi groups. The Anti-Defamation League of B'nai Brith maintains a close watch on anti-Semitic acts and trends in the country.

Most American Jews now see themselves as belonging to a historic community that is held together by faith and mutual responsibility. Though very much rooted in the United States, most American Jews look upon Israel as the spiritual center of their faith, and they feel a strong commitment to the survival of the State of Israel. Many Americans express that commitment through financial and political support, organized by groups such as Israel Bonds and the United Jewish Appeal.

Another immigrant group making their mark on the American Jewish landscape are the tens of thousands of Israelis who have left their homeland and settled in the United States. In the aftermath of the Six Day War, their numbers grew steadily. It is estimated that over eight hundred thousand Israelis now reside permanently in the United States. Some came to find new economic possibilities, others to find refuge from the ongoing political turmoil in Israel, and some simply because they were curious to see America.

In the beginning, some American Jews found it difficult to accept this new migration, perceiving them almost as traitors to Israel. But over the years, local communities have reached out to their Israeli brothers.

107

Canada

The beautiful cities and countryside of Canada are home to approximately three hundred thousand Jews. Jewish settlement started there in 1759 in Montreal. In the beginning, many Jews in Montreal were furriers and clothes makers. The streets of this European-flavored city still hold turn-of-the-century Jewish memories, and its neighborhoods retain their sentimental value for many former immigrants. Today, however, the city of Toronto houses the largest Jewish population in the country.

Canadian Jewry is mostly Orthodox and very pro-Israel. The community has managed to develop a respected system of Hebrew schools that embrace Zionist values. Unlike those in the United States, Canadian Hebrew schools managed to mold themselves successfully using the Israeli educational system as a model. The newest generations, therefore, speak Hebrew and are being raised in a spirited, Israeli-like environment.

Being a bilingual (French/English) society, the province of Quebec also attracted many Sephardic Jews, who came from the French-speaking Arabic countries of Algeria, Tunisia, and Morocco. To date, the most pressing concern of this low-profile community of both Ashkenazic and Sephardic Jews is the rise and fall of the nationalist French-Canadian party and the anti-Semitism that sometimes appears in its wake.

Latin America

Latin America became a major destination point of Jewish migration only at the end of the nineteenth century, although Sephardic Jews had settled there as early as the sixteenth century when they traveled from Amsterdam to the Brazilian port city of Recife. A small Jewish community thrived there and branched out as far as the Caribbean islands. Persecution did exist, but after the American and French revolutions, Jews began to benefit from the religious tolerance that Protestants and other minorities gained in Catholic countries.

Most of the Jewish community in Latin America today is of Ashkenazic, Eastern European origin. The parents and grandparents of these approximately six hundred and fifty thousand Jews brought with them their Yiddish culture and established communities similar to those in the United States. Argentina boasts the largest Jewish community in South America—with a Jewish population of more than two hundred thousand.

These prosperous, predominantly commerce-oriented Jews live with the uncertainty that comes from the region's endemic political instability. Too often these Jewish communities have found themselves victims of anti-Semitic uprisings, including those that parallel general uprisings and concomitant economic downturns. South American countries are also well known as refuges for Nazi war criminals, who have influenced the continued activities of neo-Nazi movements.

The warm and spirited Jews of South America have emigrated to the United States and Israel in a steady stream over the past few decades. Some kibbutzim in Israel were built by immigrants from these countries. The special flavors and customs of South America are preserved in these settlements, which are thereby enriched with Latin music and festivities reminiscent of the great carnivals in their "old country."

ABBA EBAN (1915–   )

Abba Eban, a world-renowned Jewish scholar and Israeli diplomat, was born in Capetown, South Africa, and spent most of his early years in England. A Cambridge University graduate, he has played a key role in the Zionist movement since the middle of the twentieth century, when he served as a British officer assigned to the Middle East during World War II.

Toward the end of that war, Eban settled in Jerusalem, where he developed a brilliant career as a first-rate diplomat. He served with Israel's United Nations delegation and as Ambassador to the United States. For many years, he represented the Labor Party in the Israeli Knesset and served as Israel's Foreign Minister.

Eban is fluent in several languages, including Arabic, and travels all over the world, lecturing and teaching. He appears as a regular guest on television shows and is the writer of numerous best-selling books, including a history of the Jewish people entitled *My People*.

SAMUEL BRONFMAN (1890–1971)

Born in Manitoba, Canada, Samuel Bronfman joined his father in the hotel trade and went on to become a major industrialist. He started a mail-order liquor business that he built into one of the world's largest distilleries.

Bronfman was a devoted Jewish activist who served as the president of the Canadian Jewish Congress for a quarter of a century. He was also vice president of the World Jewish Congress. A supporter of social causes, he assisted Canadian hospitals, universities, and museums. On his seventieth birthday, his four children donated the Bronfman Biblical and Archeology Wing to the Israel Museum in Jerusalem.

South Africa

The first group of Jewish settlers came to South Africa from Britain and Germany after England bought the Cape of Good Hope from the Dutch in the seventeenth century. Soon enough they prospered in this new land of opportunity and held key roles in the community, especially as exporters of wool, mohair, and wine.

After the discovery of the diamond fields, a new wave of Jewish migration reached South Africa. A group of young Londoners came to build their future in mining and polishing diamonds. These Jewish immigrants opened new businesses and turned the fledgling South African diamond industry into a world giant.

At the end of the nineteenth century, many Jews from Lithuania arrived in the country; these pragmatic, industrious Jews were extremely devoted Zionists as well as talented businessmen. Some of the newcomers moved inland to become peddlers and small-town merchants, but their children generally moved back to the larger cities and became leaders in such fields as clothing manufacturing and textiles. The third generation, as in other parts of the world, went on to enter professional fields, such as medicine and law.

Australia

Jewish emigration to Australia began in 1817. British Jews arrived first; Eastern European Jews came in later years. From the very beginning, they enjoyed religious and political freedom and managed to contribute to the economic and industrial life. Politically, Jews have succeeded in occupying major positions; for instance, Sir Isaac Isaacs served as Governor General.

THE ARAB WORLD

Although the history of Arab Jewry is a glorious one, the establishment of the State of Israel and the Arab-Israeli conflicts has for the most part driven once proud Arab Jewish communities to extinction. The presence of Jewish communities in the Arab world dates to the beginning of the Diaspora. The greatest number of Jews, however, arrived in the Middle East after 1492, following the exodus from Spain due to the Inquisition. Sephardic Jews in Arab countries developed their own distinct traditions and managed to preserve a vibrant faith even under the most difficult circumstances. When the majority of these Middle Eastern Jews moved to Israel and other countries in the twentieth century, they brought with them a wealth of cultural riches.

Egypt

There was no more picturesque and colorful Jewish community than the one that thrived in Egypt. When the Arabs conquered the country in 640 A.D., however, they found only the remnants of the great Jewish community of Alexandria, which had once been home to Talmudic scholars. These survivors had hung on since the fall of the city in the second century of the common era.

Starting with the great Jewish philosopher Moses Maimonides, who lived and worked in medieval Cairo, the Jewish community in Egypt prospered again and grew tremendously, producing influential Jewish families who contributed to almost every aspect of Egyptian life. Egypt's international standing attracted people from all over and enabled the Jews there to become cosmopolitan and well educated. The community developed into one of the richest centers of Jewish learning and commerce in the world.

Around the time of the Second World War, when Egypt, influenced by European trends, was swept by a wave of nationalism, the Jewish community numbered ninety thousand. Soon thereafter anti-Semitism became a problem, and with the establishment of the State of Israel, the Egyptian government turned against the local Jews, imprisoning and expelling large numbers of them. A great exodus began, and by 1955, the community numbered only thirty thousand.

The 1956 Sinai Campaign triggered a second migration from Egypt, when the remaining Jews, whose businesses and homes were threatened by the government, fled Egypt and turned to Israel. Today only about one hundred Jews continue to live in Egypt, most of them senior citizens who struggle to maintain the few synagogues and cemeteries.

Tunisia

The colors and traditions of Tunisian Jewry are perhaps more evident today in Israel and France than in Tunisia, as only about three thousand Jews still reside in this North African country. Jews had lived in Tunisia since ancient times and survived many changes of regime, until the advent of modern independence in 1956. That year was a turning point for this prosperous community, because Tunisia announced a nationwide plan for "Tunisification." All Jewish councils and establishments were ordered abolished, and huge riots against Jews took place throughout the country. The great synagogue of Tunis was destroyed in the riots, and the government stopped subsidizing the Jewish community. Thousands of Jews left Tunisia following its independence. All told, between 1948 and 1970 over forty thousand Tunisian Jews settled in Israel.

F. Donati   2 ⁹/₈   CAIRO

This Egyptian Jew is wearing a traditional etched robe and round hat.

111

Morocco

Morocco is host to the one surviving, healthy Jewish community in the Arab World. The history of Jews in Morocco dates back to the second century of the common era. This colorful and culturally rich community has enjoyed the support of Moroccan rulers throughout its long history. Even modern Morocco has shown great respect and support for its Jewish citizens. Although the current king supports the community in Morocco, Pan-Arab political considerations have led to the gradual outlawing of the Zionist movement, and the next king could easily disrupt the community's status and situation.

The deeply rooted traditions of Moroccan Jewry have given birth to some of the most important members of the world's Sephardic community, including many Sephardic cantors, rabbis, and communal leaders. Since the establishment of the State of Israel over 250,000 Moroccan Jews have settled there. Because of their large numbers and distinctive traditions, Moroccan Jews have had a major influence on Israel's culture, cuisine, and religion.

Yemen

The Yemenite Jewish community, which dates back at least to the days of the Second Temple, is one of the most interesting and peculiar success stories of the Jewish Diaspora. Yemenite Jews believe that their community was established after the destruction of Solomon's (First) Temple. They also believe that their sufferings were God's punishment for not returning to the Land of Israel in the days of Ezra and Nechemia. (Ezra and Nechemia, scribes and religious leaders, urged Jews to return to Judea from Babylonia, where they were in exile after the destruction of the First Temple.)

Of all the Arab Jewish communities, the Yemenites had the poorest standard of living. With only a few exceptions, Yemenite Jews were economically restricted by their rulers' excessive taxes. Despite these hardships, they built up a reputation as the best jewelers and craftsmen in Yemen.

Throughout the long years of their exile in Yemen, these Jews never gave up their faith or their hope of returning to their homeland. Amid the poverty of their surroundings, they always maintained tidy homes and managed to satisfy their desire for beauty by creating embroidered piecework, pottery, and their own music. Because they lived deep inside the country's interior, they remained cut off from foreign cultures and influences. (The port city of Aden was the one exception: Jewish merchants there learned from the modern world around them.)

Remote as they were, however, even the inland Jews heard of the birth of Zionism, and by 1948, when the State of Israel was born, over eighteen thousand Yemenite Jews were already living there. Between the years 1949 and 1950 nearly the entire Jewish population left Yemen for Israel by a special airlift called "Operation Magic Carpet." The remaining Jewish families left the country a few years later to settle in London.

This darker-skinned Jewish community differed from other immigrant groups who moved to Israel. They were unfamiliar with such trappings of modern society as electricity, toilets, running water, buses, railroads, and airplanes. Quickly bridging this cultural gap, the dedicated Yemenite people soon became one of the mainstays of modern Israeli culture, contributing their artistic vision, their humor, and their intelligence to the country as a whole.

These Yemenite children (above) are studying at a traditional school. This Yemenite girl (left) is dressed in traditional clothing with an embroidered robe and a hat covered with handmade jewelry.

113

114

This Sephardic Jew from Salonika is dressed in a typical robe and hat.

MOLLY PICON *(1898–1992)*

Born in New York, Molly Picon rose to fame in both the Yiddish and English theater. She started her dramatic career on the stages of the Second Avenue Yiddish theaters and from there became Queen of the Jewish theater.

After performing for several years with Kessler's Theater, she and her husband, Jacob Kolich, toured the world performing with a vaudeville company. In 1942 she founded the Molly Picon Theater in New York. During and after World War II, she performed in camps for displaced persons, after which she extensively toured Australia, South Africa, and Europe.

In 1960, Molly Picon came back to the English theater, playing the leading role in *A Majority of One* in London. The following year marked her Broadway success in *Milk and Honey*, and in 1967 she created the smash hit *How To Be a Jewish Mother*. In her autobiography, *So Laugh a Little*, she tells the story of her entire family.

Iran

The Jewish community of Iran remained intact longer than those in other Moslem countries. This ancient community rose from abject poverty less than fifty years ago to a position of power, wealth, and prosperity. In the years following World War II, when the Shah consolidated his power, Jewish institutions and activities had to be supported by organizations outside Iran; the country was not willing to contribute to synagogues and Jewish schools. Approximately five thousand Iranian Jews lived in a run-down ghetto in Tehran.

Today, it is estimated that about thirty thousand Jews live in Khomeini's Iran. Although the Ayatollah took away some of the liberties that the Jews had had under the Shah, they are still granted protection as one of three religious minorities in the country and enjoy complete freedom of worship. Oddly enough, the Jewish community in Iran is now in the midst of a revival. Worshipers fill the synagogues and attend more and more Jewish functions. New afternoon Hebrew schools have been established, and parents are trying to bring their children closer to Judaism. The Jewish community has had to pay a price, though, for all this freedom: it must officially condemn the State of Israel and Zionism.

The Continuing Diaspora

The Arab-Jewish Diaspora is a vanishing phenomenon. In Iraq, where over 125,000 Jews resided before 1948, there are almost no Jews left. In Libya, which was home to over thirty-eight thousand Jews, no remnants of Jewish life exist. Algerian Jews, who numbered over 140,000, fled the country to live in Israel and other countries. Some five thousand Jews still live in Syria under a shadow of fear and uncertainty, unable to leave the country.

Outside of the Middle East, the Diaspora is still evolving. Jews have lived and continue to reside all over Europe, in England, France, Turkey, Greece, Italy, and Scandinavia. India has a Jewish population. The ability to forgive and forget has even brought Jews back to Germany.

But no matter where Jews live and what occupations they take for themselves, their unity enables them to make the necessary adaptations to a new culture. Communities all over the world serve as a support system for all new Jewish immigrants and wanderers. It is a network of love and support, deeply rooted in the very beginnings of the Jewish people at Mount Sinai.

115

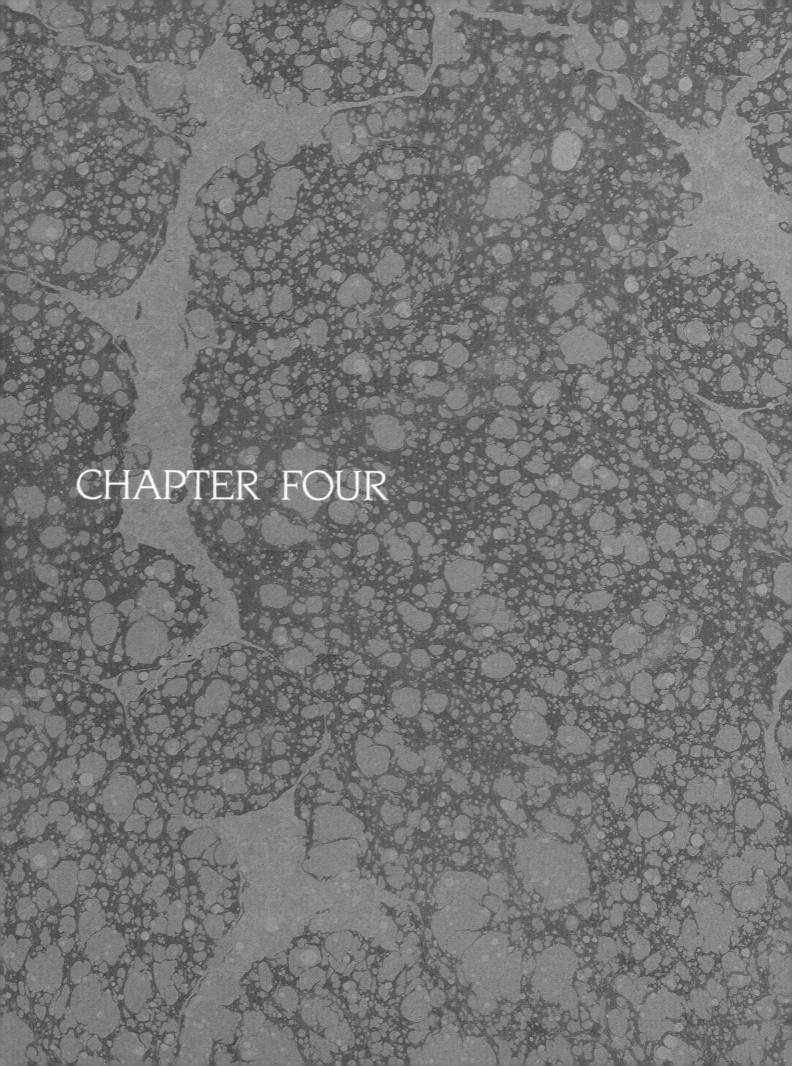

CHAPTER FOUR

ISRAEL: LAND OF MILK, HONEY, AND STRUGGLE

PHOTOGRAPHY IN THIS SECTION BY RICHARD LOBELL

We, members of the people's council, representatives of the Jewish community of Eretz-Israel and of the Zionist movement, are here assembled on the day of the termination of the British mandate over Eretz-Israel and, by virtue of our natural and historic right and on the strength of the resolution of the United Nations General Assembly, hereby declare the establishment of a Jewish state in Eretz-Israel, to be known as the State of Israel. . . . The State of Israel will be open for Jewish immigration and for the Ingathering of the Exiles; it will foster the development of the country for the benefit of all its inhabitants; it will be based on freedom, justice, and peace as envisaged by the prophets of Israel. . . . Placing our trust in the Rock of Israel, we affix our signatures to this proclamation at this session of the provisional Council of State, on the soil of the Homeland, in the city of Tel-Aviv, on the Sabbath eve, the 5th day of Iyar, 5708 (14th May, 1948). —Israel's Declaration of Independence

The proclamation of Israel's independence changed the Jewish world and the world's perception of Judaism. On the exciting, emotional Sabbath when David Ben-Gurion read the announcement in his sharp, determined voice, world Jewry entered a new era. Israel had become a refuge for every Jew and an inspiration for Jewish communities all over the world. Israel's existence has been a miracle in the desert, a manifestation of courageous human spirit.

The establishment of the State of Israel gave birth to a new type of Jew. The typical Israeli is a strong human being, deeply rooted in the soil of his country, stripped of the manners, thoughts, and behaviors that were typical of the Diaspora Jew. For one thing, sabras—native Israelis—do not feel the need to tout their Judaism publicly, as Jews might in another country.

Israel's relationship with world Jewry has always been complex. Although Jews around the world understand the importance of Israel's existence, few American and Western European Jews have moved to Israel. The security, comfort, and adopted traditions of life in the West have proved more compelling than life in Israel. Still, knowing that there is a homeland that awaits every Jew unconditionally warms the Diaspora and encourages Jews throughout the world to support Israel both morally and financially.

The land of milk and honey also attracts visitors, scholars, and students. People of all faiths come to Israel to see the flourishing desert and to observe the ancient religious and historical sites. Israel welcomes visitors and proudly shows its wonders to all curious and adventurous souls.

THE LAND

Israel is a small country. About the size of New Jersey, it measures only 260 miles (418.4km) long and 70 miles (112.6km) at its widest part. It forms part of the bridge between Africa and Eurasia. The country lies between the desert to the east and south and the Mediterranean Sea to the west. These two great forces—desert and sea—have determined the diversity of this little country's climate and landscape.

Tiny as it is, the ancient land of Israel boasts hills and curving valleys that hold the stories of thousands of years of adventure. The biblical past is spread throughout its deserts and mountains. The land echoes a time when history was created in war and in peace, in love and in hatred. Voices of the great prophets still hang in the air, and at night, if one listens closely, King David's harp might be heard humming in the dark.

But from the ancient past, a bright and distinct present rises, manifested in each and every corner of the land. This mixture of past and present creates an extravagant picture: the Land of Israel.

The Northern Waters

The Kinneret, or the Sea of Galilee, does not resemble any North American lake. Any attempt to compare it to one of the Great Lakes or even to Lake Powell in Utah is doomed to fail, as the deep blue Kinneret is only fourteen miles (22km) long and seven and a half miles (12km) wide. Yet no other lake in the world has had as many songs, poems, and stories written about it as the Kinneret. Israelis liken the lake to a beautiful woman.

Located in the northeast corner of the country, the Kinneret is near the borders of Syria and Jordan. To the west rise the rocky hills of the Lower Galilee; to the east one can see the volcanic cliffs of the Golan Heights. To the south, like a long, beautiful hazel tail, flows the Jordan River. At night, when the kibbutzim around the Kinneret light their tiny lights and fishermen spread their nets on the water, an enchanting spirit envelops the Queen of Galilee.

Tourists and countrymen who visit the Kinneret find lodging and food in Tiberias, the only city along the lake's shores. Every weekend this historic town fills with vacationers who swim, water-ski, or travel the mile and a half (2.4km) to the hottest mineral springs in Israel, which gush out of the earth at 140°F (60°C). The therapeutic waters draw visitors from all over the world.

119

The city of Tiberias sits on the shore of the Kinneret (the Sea of Galilee).

ISAAC STERN *(1920–)*

The world-renowned violinist Isaac Stern was born in the Ukraine and came as a child to San Francisco, where his mother worked as a pianist and teacher. At the age of eight, he took up the violin, and at eleven, he played with the San Francisco Orchestra under conductor Pierre Monteux. His great fame came after World War II when he started playing concerts all over the world, both solo and with such fine artists as cellist Pablo Casals.

Stern is active in other endeavors as well and played a major part in the movement that saved New York's Carnegie Hall from destruction. He is president of the Carnegie Hall Foundation as well as the America-Israel Culture Foundation. Stern visits and performs in Israel frequently and is an enthusiastic sponsor of Israeli artists abroad.

Tall eucalyptus trees stand erect along the winding road circling the Kinneret, spreading their shade over its waters. While driving along the shores of the lake, travelers pass Deganya, the oldest kibbutz in Israel. Founded in 1909 by a group of Jews who had grown tired of the daily persecutions they suffered in Europe, Deganya exemplified a new way of life, where the needs of society come before the needs of the individual. In their promised land, these immigrants built a democratic community based on equality and mutual help. After the birth of Deganya, many other kibbutzim settled in the area, nestled among beautiful views of the Kinneret and the Golan Heights. For many years these kibbutzim were targets of Syrian attacks. Since the Six Day War and the Israeli conquest of the Golan Heights, these settlements have had a chance to prosper and flourish on the fruitful northern soil.

To North Americans familiar with such rivers as the Hudson and the Mississippi, the Jordan River may seem like a small stream. Yet because of its rich folk history, it attracts visitors from all over the world. Christians believe that Jesus was baptized in the Jordan River, and thousands of followers make a pilgrimage each year to the baptism site at the entrance to Kibbutz Kinneret. Quietly, the Jordan flows through the Kinneret in the north and into the Dead Sea in the south. This magnificent sliver of water forms the natural borderline between Israel and Jordan once it departs the Kinneret.

Northern Israel above the Kinneret presents the most exquisite, well-watered part of this contradictory land. The Upper Galilee provides spectacular scenery and fascinating historical sites that stand in bold contrast to the nearby modern settlements.

The winding narrow road from the lower Galilee to Safad, the crown of the Galilee, runs through a valley of ancient olive trees, some believed to be as old as two thousand years. In biblical times, this was the kingdom of the ancient tribe of Ahser, the oil suppliers to the temple.

Large pine forests spread along the road up to the peak, where the city of Safad reveals itself. Safad was built during the great revolt against the Romans in the years 66 to 70 of the common era. Sixteen hundred years ago, in Talmudic times, the summit of the hill became an important site; bonfires built on its top announced the beginning of a new month, thereby determining the Jewish calendar. Through the ages, the city has known endless catastrophes: earthquakes, riots, and conquests.

As one passes through the cobbled streets of the old Jewish section of Safad, ancient synagogues can still be seen. Among them are Rabbi Yosef Caro's home of prayer and learning. Rabbi Caro was the author of the *Shulchan Aruch*, one of the most authoritative handbooks of Jewish practices. Nearby stands the home of Rabbi Isaac Luria, founding father of Jewish mysticism (the Kabbalah).

Great folk stories have always been associated with Safad and its Jewish community. One traditional story recounts that in the great earthquake of 1837,

120

ARTHUR MILLER (1915–   )

Arthur Miller received his education in Michigan. He began writing in the late 1930s, although his early career was in editing. He didn't acquire a worldwide reputation until after World War II, when he wrote his first two plays and a novel, *Focus*, that dealt with anti-Semitism. The year 1947 brought him great success with *All My Sons*, but it was *Death of a Salesman* that won him a Pulitzer Prize and worldwide recognition.

The 1950s and the McCarthy era provoked Miller to oppose restraints on freedom of speech, and in his 1953 play *The Crucible*, he used the 1692 Salem witch trials to speak out against McCarthy's anti-Communist campaign. *A View From the Bridge* earned him another Pulitzer Prize, after which he wrote the screenplay *The Misfits*.

Miller returned to the stage with his autobiographical play *After the Fall*, based on his life with Marilyn Monroe, from whom he was divorced in 1961. His authentic and deep drama is internationally famous and has been translated into many languages. His dramatic portrayal of contemporary American life has made him one of the most important playwrights living today.

Kibbutzim in the hills overlooking the Kinneret were among the earliest settlements in Israel. Fields of olive and avocado trees form a patchwork on the landscape.

YOSSEL BERGNER (1920–)

Son of Yiddish poet and essayist Melech Ravitch, Yossel Bergner is one of Israel's finest painters. Born in Vienna and raised in Warsaw, he immigrated to Australia in 1937 and finally settled with his painter wife, Audrey, in Israel in 1951. His first period in Israel was spent in Safad, where he painted expressionist scenes of bright walls with windows and strange figures. Bergner's later paintings describe the emotional world of the early Russian settlers in Palestine; he placed nineteenth-century figures wearing sophisticated clothes in Middle Eastern settings. After 1961 his paintings became more abstract, but his emotional colors have never changed. Bergner, who also designed many theater sets for Israeli theater companies, is one of the most popular Jewish painters in the world.

YESHAYAHU LEIBOWITZ (1903–)

Israeli scientist and scholar Yeshayahu Leibowitz was born in Riga, Latvia. He studied chemistry, philosophy, and medicine, and in 1935, he moved to Palestine to become a professor of biochemistry and neurophysiology at the Hebrew University in Jerusalem. His fields of research include saccharides and enzymes in chemistry and the nervous system of the heart in physiology. In addition, Professor Leibowitz is a researcher in the history and philosophy of science.

His uncompromising approach and strong language have made him one of the most controversial personalities in both secular and religious circles. Leibowitz sees Judaism as a religious and historical phenomenon characterized by the recognition of the duty to serve God according to the Jewish law. Leibowitz believes that the service of God is for its own sake, without the need to achieve any other goals or improvements in one's life.

He is a great supporter of separation between religion and state and after the Six Day War fiercely rejected the annexation of the occupied territories.

122

when most of the Sephardic synagogue was ruined, the wall containing the Holy Ark was miraculously spared. The community built another Ark to use during the year, saving the original for use only on the Days of Awe and Shavuot. Believers suggest that anyone who disobeys this custom will be cursed, like the twelve men who had to remove the ancient Torah scrolls for renovations and died soon after. Even the greatest skeptics may want to don some blue—believed to be protection against evil spirits, because blue is the color of heaven—before walking through Safad's spooky and mysterious alleys.

On the hillside below Safad lies the old cemetery, the final resting place of many of the great Kabbalists. (Kabbalists were an important group of Jews who dealt with mystical philosophy and practice. The chief questions raised by the Kabbalists focused on the nature of God, the creation of the universe, and the destiny of man and the world.) Thousands of people come to pray at the gravesite of their spiritual heroes. Many of these modern-day pilgrims believe that each Kabbalist has specific powers that can still help them achieve their goals in life. Bus loads of both young and old make their way every day to Safad to ask for mercy and goodwill from their beloved *tzadikim* (righteous men): girls who want to marry, or marry well; women who ask for a cure to their illnesses; men who beg for food for their families. At night, the deserted graveyard looks like a large haunted ghost town twinkling with burning candles left behind by believers.

Safad also boasts a legendary swimming pool. Fed by natural springs from the surrounding mountains, it is believed that its water makes people look younger. It's no wonder that this pool is so crowded during the summer months!

After the birth of modern Israel, many artists came to live here, drawn by its mysticism and cool weather. Both the city and its heroic-looking mountains inspired those who came. In turn, they added a new dimension to life in Safad.

Safad, the crown of the Galilee, is an ancient city that has known endless catastrophes through the ages: earthquakes, riots, and conquests.

Many of the painters and sculptors have left in recent years, however, now that the city has again become the religious town it once was.

Traveling north, passing Rosh Pina, Hatzor, the Hula Valley, Kiryat Shmona, and Metulah, one arrives at Tel Dan. Shaded by large trees, this ice-cold spring is one of the sources of the Jordan River. An Arabic legend tells how three rivers—Hatzbani, Banias, and Dan—argued between themselves as to which was the most important. The Lord himself came down to judge and, after hearing their arguments, pronounced his judgment: "You should unite, and then you will become the most important river!" They did, and became the Jordan River.

Since the Six Day War, new roads connect the Dan to the Banias waterfall on the lower levels of the Golan Heights. There, a panoramic view vies with the beautifully winding roads themselves, which take visitors all the way to Mount Hermon and the stretched half-moon-shaped Golan Heights. Deep canyons, streams, waterfalls, rich vegetation, and hiking trails define the area. Ancient burial sites lie side by side with reminders of more recent wars and heroic fights. New kibbutzim, *moshavim* (settlements), and even one city, Katzrim, populate the heights and overlook a mesmerizing view of the Kinneret.

Part of Mount Hermon, the highest mountain in Israel at 9,000 feet (2,743m), was incorporated into the State of Israel after the Six Day War in 1967. Since then, skiing attracts thousands of visitors throughout the winter months.

Overleaf: The many faces of Israel.

126

Nahal Audat (top), near Sde Boker, is one of the many dry riverbeds that crisscross the Negev Desert. In a scene that evokes the life of the ancient Israelites (above), a Bedouin shepherdess tends her flock in the desert.

MARTIN BUBER *(1878–1965)*

Martin Buber, a religious philosopher and scholar, was well known as an interpreter of Hasidism—the eighteenth-century pietistic movement of Jews who believed in the power and centrality of prayer and devotion to God in the spiritual life of the Jews. Born and educated in Vienna, he became editor of an important Zionist publication, *Die Welt*, and fled when the Nazis came to power. After coming to Israel, he was appointed a professor at the Hebrew University in Jerusalem.

Buber was an enthusiastic supporter of the pioneer settlement movement in Israel, and he used his writing to promote Zionism. His main academic work, however, was dedicated to the study of Hasidism, investigating and interpreting the sources and spiritual achievements of this Jewish movement. For Buber, the essence of religious life was not the affirmation of religious belief but the way in which a person related to others and met the challenges of everyday life. He lectured throughout the world and distinguished himself as one of the great leaders of his generation for both Christians and Jews.

The Negev

Empty space. The open frontier. The wilderness of the Negev desert in the south of Israel encompasses about half the land. Although it is mostly uninhabited, vast parts of this virgin land have been developed in the last twenty years. Green buds, little towns with red roofs, kibbutzim, and settlements now flourish in the hot sands where water is piped into the desert. The Negev tells the story of people successfully taming nature.

The warm, dry Negev has a varied landscape: sand, dust, mountains, and canyons. It is home to a great variety of animals and plants. The desert has also harbored nomad tribes since ancient times. It has never gone through such tremendous changes as it did after the birth of Israel in 1948, when pioneers declared their determination to conquer this hot, empty, almost impossible land. Even a few of the wandering Bedouin tribes decided to settle down.

Be'er Sheva, the capital of the Negev, is a modern and vital town on the northern border of the desert, with more than 100,000 citizens. Ancient history tells us that thousands of years ago, Abraham, coming up from Egypt, dug a well (*be'er*) here for his thirsty flock. The modern city still has camels strolling down the street and a Bedouin market day every Thursday. The wilderness and frontier-town feel in Be'er Sheva exist side by side with a new and almost futuristic-looking university and ancient archeological digs.

Driving almost due south along the Negev's roads, roughly paralleling the border of the Sinai Peninsula, the beauty of the desert is revealed. It is not unusual to see animals making their way to water supplies, always wary of unwanted human visitors. After a long ride through the empty desert, the city of Eilat appears. Located on the shores of the Red Sea, Eilat, the southernmost Israeli city, lies between Egypt's Sinai Peninsula to the west and Jordan to the east. It is a favorite winter vacation resort. Tall red mountains surround the city and its small buildings. Hotels and beaches dot the shores, and clean, cool water refreshes bathers in the hot, dry air of Eilat throughout the year.

Divers proclaim the deep blue waters of the Red Sea to be the best in the world. The Coral Beach Nature Reserve provides a fascinating glimpse of an amazing underwater world for both divers and visitors who break the surface of the water. At night, the lights of the Jordanian city of Aqaba can be seen across the sea like thousands of bright eyes in the dark. Aqaba, the biblical port of Etzion Gaber, was King Solomon's outlet to Africa and the port where the Queen of Sheba landed.

127

MENACHEM BEGIN *(1913–1992)*

The former commander of the secret Jewish national military organization (IZL) and Israel's Prime Minister during the war with Lebanon in 1983, Menachem Begin received a Nobel Peace Prize for his participation in negotiating and signing the Camp David peace treaty with Egypt. Born in Poland, Begin graduated from the Law School of the University of Warsaw and then joined Betar, the right-wing Zionist youth movement. When the Germans invaded Warsaw, he escaped to Vilna, where he was arrested by the Soviet authorities. They accused him of anti-Soviet activity and sentenced him to eight years of hard labor in the Arctic region. Begin was released because of his Polish citizenship and arrived in Palestine in 1942.

After finishing his army service, Begin became the commander of the IZL and led the underground in armed warfare against the British Mandatory Government. In 1948, he formed the Herut party, the main opposition party in the Israeli Knesset for many years. In 1967, before the Six Day War, he was invited to join the Government of National Unity and was made a Minister without Portfolio. Subsequently leading his party for a first-time victory over the ruling Labor party, Begin became Israel's Prime Minister and went on to sign the peace treaty at Camp David with the Egyptians. Following the war with Lebanon, Begin resigned from politics.

The Judean Desert (Midbar Yehuda)

Only a short drive from Jerusalem, hot, dry desert air welcomes the escapee from the city. Striking desert landscapes, flourishing oases, and ancient cultures buried in the sand hide within the Judean Desert. Located 1,300 feet (396.2m) below sea level, the Dead Sea, the lowest place in the world, is also found here.

Light brown mountaintops with trees sprinkled here and there capture the eye in this picturesque site. Camels wander freely as if they have no owners. Signs en route point the way to old monasteries. And green blankets cover the riverbeds here in the midst of the desert. In the distance, the Dead Sea shimmers.

The Dead Sea is famous for its health benefits. The salt of the sea is believed to cure back pains and rheumatic disorders. Thousands of tourists come here to dip in the mineral springs and mud baths. Stories of ancient societies unfold in the ruins of such nearby archeological sites as the Qumran caves, where the Dead Sea Scrolls were found. The remains of the city of the Essenes—a Jewish semi-monastic community whose members lived around the time of Jesus—is located here. Sitting by the water, watching the red mountains in the distance at sunset, is a unique and unforgettable experience.

Here, too, towers the clifftop fortress of Masada, which at first sight does not look particularly special. But for Israelis and Jews everywhere it is a symbol of freedom. Masada holds within its ruins the story of a small group of Jews who retreated to the dry mountaintop to fight the Romans after the destruction of Jerusalem in the year 70 of the common era. Upon seeing that the effort to defend themselves from the Roman soldiers was doomed, 967 men, women, and children, led by Elazar Ben Yair, apparently decided to take their own lives. They kissed one another for the last time. Ten men were chosen to slash the throats of the others; one of them then killed the nine remaining martyrs and finally took his own life. Two women and five children hid and survived to tell the story.

Almost every month, Israeli soldiers proclaim, "Masada will never fall again," in a ceremony atop the mountain. The remains of the fortress are visited by thousands of tourists each year, and weddings and bar mitzvahs are also celebrated here, for the magnificent view from the top of the fortress provides a panoramic scene of both the sea and the desert. Masada is a symbol of both hope and despair in the life of the nation.

The brown, barren hills of the Judean Desert, where David fled from Saul's anger, roll down from Jerusalem to Jericho and the Dead Sea.

130

This aerial photograph (above) shows King Herod's mountain fortress, where well-stocked storerooms and an elaborate system of aqueducts allowed the zealots to resist Roman forces.

The Dead Sea (opposite, top), with Jordan in the background, can be seen from Ein Fescha.

Masada (left) is a symbol of Israel's unbreakable will to remain a proud and sovereign nation.

The Temple (above) is in the center of Jerusalem.

The Great Cities

Jerusalem

A steep hill. The car climbs up along a winding road that passes through forests of pine trees that remain a green vision all year long. Crossing Sha'ar Hagai, the Gate to the Valley, travelers can see the rusting remains of burned vehicles left as a reminder of the 1948 siege when an Arab ambush attacked. High rocks rise on either side of the road, guarding the traveler on his way to the holy city. After a long curve, a glow in the sun, like a crown, appears. White as snow, the first buildings of the City of David come into sight. Jerusalem.

She is called Jerusalem of Gold, the Eternal City, the City of David, the City of Light, Zion, and the City of Peace (which is what Jerusalem means in Hebrew). She is a city that rises above the rest of the world. Scholars and archeologists date the city as far back as five thousand years. Many ancient maps place Jerusalem at the center of the world, and when visiting its many religious sites, it is easy to understand why.

Jerusalem, however, is also a modern city, bustling in its everyday life. Most of its Jewish citizens are fierce patriots who consider all other cities inferior. Jerusalem ignites the emotions visually and viscerally. The mixture of religions and people, old and new, makes Jerusalem a unique city. Surprisingly, despite the tremendous diversity of population and the changes Jerusalem has experienced since its reunification in 1967, it is still an intimate place.

This drawing of the Temple of Salomon in Jerusalem is from a Moravian Haggadah *that dates back to 1729.*

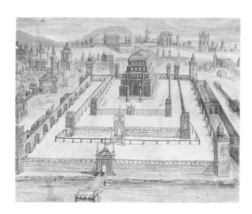

The Old City of Jerusalem can be seen with the Mount Scopus campus of the Hebrew University in the background.

It is almost impossible to condense the history of this ancient city, which is important to three major religions: Judaism, Christianity, and Islam. It is a history that has been written in blood. Events that changed the world occurred here. King David built up the city as the capital of his kingdom in the year 1000 B.C.E. King Solomon built the Temple of God here. Then in 586 B.C.E., the Babylonians destroyed the city and the Temple was razed.

The exiled Jews in Babylon remembered Zion (Jerusalem), and many returned, beginning in the sixth century B.C.E., to rebuild it and once again make it the capital of the Jewish nation with the Second Temple as its center. The Romans conquered the city in 70 C.E. and destroyed the Temple and Jerusalem, rebuilding it as a pagan Roman city. In the years that passed, more than thirty conquests passed the city from one ruler to the next; each government dictated the city's way of life in a different manner and left traces that can still be seen in the many archeological and architectural remains in the Old City.

A model of the Second Temple stands in the Holyland Hotel in Jerusalem.

134

Behind sixteenth-century Turkish walls lies an authentic nineteenth-century city: the Old City of Jerusalem. A great mixture of historical remnants crowds into 220 acres (89ha): Arab shrines, crusader churches, Herodian walls, Byzantine columns, and Mamluk buildings. The sound of the muezzin, a Moslem who calls his people to prayer, is mixed here with the sounds of church bells. Arab women carrying loads of produce on their heads walk through extremely narrow cobblestone alleys filled with playing children. The Arab market, too, paints a colorful picture.

Jews were forced out of the Old City of Jerusalem after the War of Independence in 1948, and the city was divided; West Jerusalem was in Israeli hands and East Jerusalem was controlled by Jordan. In 1967, reunification opened the gates of the Old City to Jews from all over the world.

Within the Old City stands a strong, heavily built two-thousand-year-old wall: the (Western) Wall, the *Kotel*. It is all that remains of the four walls that surrounded the Second Temple, which stood on Mount Moriah. Over the years, the precise location of the Temple was lost. When the city's gates were once again opened to Jews, they wouldn't dare step too near the site of the Holy Temple, because the ground was sacred, and since the destruction of the Second Temple, Jews were forbidden to walk on the holy earth there. The closest Jews could approach was the Western Wall, which enabled them to pray as close as possible to the sanctuary without entering the sacred Temple Mount. It became the place to mourn the destruction of the House of the Lord and over the years has turned into a symbol of Jewish hope for rebuilding the ancient Kingdom of Israel.

The Western Wall, the Kotel, is all that remains of the four walls that surrounded the Second Temple. Here, Jews can come closest to the glory of ancient Israel.

Many Israelis who lived through the Six Day War vividly remember Colonel Uzi Narkis, commander of the Jerusalem operation, announcing on the radio: "Temple Mount is in our hands. Temple Mount is in our hands." Two minutes later, Rabbi Shlomo Goren blew the shofar for the first time in years by the Western Wall, opening a new era of Jewish worship in Jerusalem. Since then, thousands of Jews make their way every day to pray by the beloved Wall and to insert little prayer notes between the Wall's huge stones. Every Friday evening, at sundown, hundreds of yeshiva (seminary) students come to the Wall to dance and sing, celebrating the holy Sabbath. Every Monday, Thursday, and Saturday bar mitzvah celebrations are held by the Wall. Each celebration deepens its symbolism of past glory and future redemption.

The Jewish Quarter in the Old City is now a renovated neighborhood, restored after the reunification of the city to absorb those Jews who wished to return to their ancestors' home. It was rebuilt to preserve the atmosphere and style of building of the Old City; any new buildings must harmonize with the original architecture.

Christians also tread through the alleys of the Old City, worshiping and following Jesus' last path. Moslems, too, come to visit the Temple Mount, atop of which lies the spectacular golden mosque, the Dome of the Rock, believed by Moslems to be the place where Mohammed rose up to heaven. A late afternoon trip to the top of the wall that surrounds the Old City provides an unforgettable sight: The last rays of the twilight sun cling to the golden cape of the Moslem shrine while green mountains spread their shade on the fading day in the holiest city in the world.

The new city (West Jerusalem) is built out of Jerusalem stone, a white stone found in the mountains around the city, and offers its own attractions: the Israel Museum, with its eclectic collection of fine arts from all over the world; the Israeli Knesset (parliament), an extraordinary architectural feat; and Yad Vashem, the memorial shrine to the six million Jews who were killed in the Holocaust, which offers an emotional trip into a horrifying past.

But perhaps the most fascinating site in this contradictory and multiethnic city is the section called Mea Shearim. Entering this neighborhood is like wandering into a strange and different world. It is the home of the Neturei Karta, an ultra-Orthodox Jewish sect that lives as if it were still in the eighteenth century. Men dressed in long black coats and wearing large-brimmed hats pass quickly in the streets, always rushing to study the Torah and the Talmud. Long beards and side curls cover their serious faces.

Women here cover themselves from head to toe. Married women shave their heads and wear head scarves, as hair is considered seductive. Before the Sabbath, women prepare the meal for the holy day, while men rush home from the *mikveh* (ritual bath). The roads to the neighborhood are closed, and nonreligious visitors are not welcome. Interestingly enough, though living within the State of Israel, these Jews are anti-Zionist and do not recognize the State. They speak only Yiddish, for they consider Hebrew a holy language to be spoken only when the Messiah comes (and in prayer).

Lag Baomer celebrations are always festive in Jerusalem.

The last rays of the summer sun bake Jerusalem (top), both old and new, in golden light.
The great synagogue, Beit Haknesset Hagadol (above), is located in Jerusalem.

138

In the market in old Jerusalem (top), Arab merchants sell their goods to both tourists and Israelis, and in the Mahane Yehuda market (above), Israeli merchants sell fruits, vegetables, and meats to city dwellers.

DAVID BEN-GURION *(1886–1973)*

David Ben-Gurion, a brilliant politician and scholar, played an important role in the establishment of the State of Israel and was Israel's first Prime Minister. To a great degree his determination made the birth of the country possible.

Ben-Gurion was born in Poland and moved to Palestine at the age of twenty. Soon after, he became involved in political activities as leader of the Labor Zionist Movement. This led to his expulsion from Palestine by the Turkish government. He then went to the United States where he organized the Jewish Legion, in which he served during World War I.

Following the occupation of Palestine by the British, Ben-Gurion moved to London, where he served as chairman and executive director of the Jewish Agency for Palestine. After the United Nations partitioned Palestine in 1947, Ben-Gurion, with others, wrote the Declaration of Independence of the Jewish State. During the War of Indepen-

dence, he led the new country as Prime Minister and Secretary of Defense.

A few years after the War of Independence, Ben-Gurion left his governmental position and moved to a new kibbutz in the southern Negev called Sdeh Boker, inspiring young families to move to this forgotten yet important part of Israel. In 1955, called back to serve his political followers, he headed the Mapai party and the government of Israel for several more years.

David Ben-Gurion was not only a political leader but a true scholar and journalist. He was one of the world's experts on the subject of the Bible and was an authority on Greek philosophy, Buddhism, and the philosophy of Spinoza—subjects on which he published numerous articles and books. A colorful figure in world politics, Ben-Gurion led a modest life with his devoted wife, Pola, and served as a role model to a renewing nation. Until the end of his life he lived in Sdeh Boker; he was buried in his beloved Negev soils.

EPHRAIM KISHON *(1924–)*

Ephraim Kishon is an Israeli satirist, playwright, film writer, and director who was born in Hungary and studied sculpture and painting at the University of Budapest, where he published numerous essays and stage pieces. Soon after moving to Israel in 1949, Kishon learned Hebrew and began writing a regular satirical column in the Israeli daily newspa-

per *Ma'Ariv,* which became one of the most popular newspaper features in the country. He also writes for the theater and the silver screen. Kishon's feature films, which he writes and directs, have been international successes; they include *Sallah* and *Arvinka.* His work has been translated into many languages, including English, French, and Spanish. Since his great success on the European stage, he divides his time between Israel and Switzerland.

GOLDA MEIR *(1898–1978)*

Golda Meir, one of the most distinguished figures in Zionism and modern Jewish history, rose to be Israel's fourth Prime Minister. Meir was born in Kiev, Russia, and immigrated with her parents to Milwaukee, Wisconsin, at the age of eight. In 1917, she married Meir Meyerson, and four years later, the couple moved to Palestine to settle in kibbutz Merhaviah. At a very early stage in her new life in Israel, Golda Meir demonstrated strong leadership qualities. She played major roles in the Political Department of the Jewish Agency, the Histadrut (Israel's Workers Union), and the Mapai party, which she helped create. She left the kibbutz to pursue her political career.

Modest in manner, Golda Meir led her party and her country through many rough times and was

famous for conducting important meetings from the kitchen of her home in Ramat Aviv. The combination of her tough political approach and motherly touch made her a unique figure in world politics. She initiated diplomatic relations with many African countries, creating a strong system of assistance for those underdeveloped nations.

Golda Meir also served as Israel's first Ambassador to Moscow, as Minister of Labor, and as Foreign Minister. She was Israel's Prime Minister during the dark, horrifying period of the Yom Kippur War. After the war, she faced accusations from bereaved parents who had lost their sons in the war and who blamed her for not being sufficiently prepared for the Arab attack. Following that great trauma she retired from politics but continued to influence Israeli political life from her little Tel Aviv kitchen. She passed away after a long struggle with cancer.

Tel Aviv

Approaching Ben-Gurion airport in Tel Aviv by plane, the city appears as a long blue coastline, punctuated with tall hotel buildings and crowded white beaches. The story of the largest city in Israel began in 1909, when a group of Jewish settlers came from the neighboring city of ancient Jaffa with the idea of building the first Jewish city on the dunes to the north.

140

It was in this city that Gymnasia Hertzelia, the first modern Hebrew high school, was built. Tel Aviv was also the first city to host a Hebrew theater, "Habima"; a port, which has since closed; and a center for artistic development in the Jewish state. Called "the city that never sleeps," Tel Aviv proudly boasts theaters, cinemas, entertainment centers, bars, coffeehouses, and restaurants—and a hip Israeli clientele for all of them.

Dizengoff, the unique main street of the city, resounds with a modern, noisy, free-spirited beat, especially in the summertime. Sidewalk coffee shops lure passersby with cold drinks and interesting people to watch. On Friday afternoons, when work ceases for the Sabbath, Dizengoff spills over with strolling youngsters, who stop to chat and seem to all know one another. In the middle of Dizengoff Circle stands a huge fountain made by sculptor Ya'acov Agam that explodes at night in a multimedia show of water, fire, sound, movement, and color. Those who prefer the beach can always walk down the Tayelet—the boardwalk—along the sea until it's time to go home to sleep before going out again to celebrate the weekend.

Tel Aviv's museums vary from the Ha'aretz Museum of Archeology and History and the Tel Aviv Museum for the Arts to the Diaspora Museum at the heart of Tel Aviv University, which displays artifacts of Jewish life from throughout the world. For those interested in folklore, the outdoor Carmel Market displays inexpensive merchandise of all kinds and is a colorful sight. Fruits and vegetables, beautifully set out and freshly picked, are sold by merchants who advertise their goods by calling out loud and raucous rhymes.

The Tel Aviv Museum of Arts, which holds exhibitions of Israeli and foreign modern artists, is also used for special performances and events.

Tel Aviv rests on the shores of the Mediterranean Sea.

143

Jaffa is a city where Arabs and Jewish artists live together.

The Aladin restaurant in the old city of Jaffa overlooks the Mediterranean Sea.

Three miles (4.8km) south of Tel Aviv lies beautiful Jaffa, a picturesque city with the oldest port in the world. Old Arab houses stand as magnificent havens for those who want to live within the glory of the past yet do not want to give up the fast pace of the present. It is a charmingly restored city.

Jaffa is a mixed town where Arabs and Jewish artists live together as good neighbors. Old church bells blend in with the sounds of the muezzin.

Jaffa's restaurants serve delicious fresh fish, usually fried on an open fire. One can eat a Middle Eastern feast while listening to a musician play the *oud*, an Arabic stringed instrument. In the summertime, many artistic festivals take place here, where the cliffs and old houses serve as a natural and enchanting background.

Haifa

The city of Haifa is like a picture etched into the cliffs over the Mediterranean and the woods of Mount Carmel. The city is built on three levels: Downtown is the Old City and the port; Hadar is a residential and shopping area; and Carmel, at the top of the mountain, consists of modern and expensive houses.

In Israel they say that Jerusalem studies, Tel Aviv dances, and Haifa works. Indeed, Haifa, the blue-collar city, is Israel's major port and contains the largest industrial area in the country. But with all of the vibrant changes that Israel has gone through, Haifa has also come a long way. The university on the top of the mountain, the Technion (Israel Technological Institute), and the Haifa Theater group have changed the image of Haifa from a "sleeping city" to a more vital one, with good music, theater, and nightclubs. Mount Carmel is also the home of an impressive building—the Bahai Shrine—surrounded by Persian gardens. In the evening, just before sundown, the last rays fall on top of the shrine's gold-leaf cap, which reflects a sharp yellow light around the area.

Haifa's greatest success story, however, lies in the remarkably good relationship between its Jewish and Arab inhabitants. Sharing the same apartment buildings and neighborhoods, Hebrew-speaking Arabs and Jews here have managed to maintain peaceful relations.

145

The top of the Bahai Shrine in Haifa is surrounded by the Persian Gardens.

THE PEOPLE

Exquisitely beautiful. Very controversial. Ancient and new. Rich and poor. All are true descriptions of the tiny land between the sea and the desert. Although Israel possesses no real natural resources, it can boast of one huge treasure, a gift that cannot be found among the earth's minerals. This resource does not come from the strong mountaintops or the deep desert sands, and yet it provides a source of true energy. It is spread all over the State of Israel and constitutes the real secret of the country—and that resource is Israel's people.

Arriving in Israel by plane, a traveler will almost inevitably be approached by a tanned, smiling young man who will offer any kind of advice, whether needed or not. Without being asked, a true sabra will offer to help carry your bag and even invite you to his home. If you are American, he or she will probably try to teach you about life in the United States and convince you that you don't know a thing about democracy. Stubborn yet warm, arrogant but giving, funny but serious, this "typical" Israeli is a direct product of the melting pot that is Israel. The new-old country blends many colors, shapes, and tastes. No single Israeli household resembles another, yet they are all united through their being Jewish. Groups from different countries who came to Israel have maintained many of their old, and sometimes even ancient, rituals. Over the years, however, as new generations joined the older groups and more and more inter-sect marriages have occurred, a fresh, original culture has been created. It is a culture that changes almost every day as Jews throughout the world continue to come to Israel to live.

The largest ethnic group in Israel comes from North Africa. Israel is home to Jewish groups from Morocco, Iraq, Iran, Tunisia, Libya, Egypt, Lebanon, Turkey, and Yemen. Each group has brought its own customs, behaviors, foods, and points of view, and some have managed to settle into Israeli life more successfully than others. Now a minority, European Jews—Russian, Polish, Romanian, German, Scandinavian—controlled the political, social, and cultural life of Israel until recently. Many immigrants from the Arab world have questioned whether they have had a fair chance in the country. It is too soon to determine the answer, but it is true that the generations who were born and raised in Israel have managed, to a large extent, to overcome the differences rooted in their origins. Israeli society is still in the process of establishing itself. It combines the culture of older generations with an entirely new younger culture that is heavily influenced by the Middle East as well as the West.

The variety of cultures that make up Israel has contributed to the creation of a colorful country. Foods from all over the world are served not only in restaurants, but also in homes. Marriages between North African Jews and European Jews give birth not only to interesting-looking children, but also to new flavors in food and new modes of behavior.

Unfortunately, not all of the differences have been settled. Differing religious beliefs have created severe conflicts in Israel, with each group trying to guard and defend its point of view. The multiethnic experiment that is Israel is still in progress, and the details of cultural integration are still being worked through. The success of Israeli unity is most apparent during troublesome times. The nation must then become one strong group of people, working and helping each other. All cultural differences and misunderstandings must disappear so the new society can truly be one nation.

GERSHOM SCHOLEM *(1897–1982)*

A leading scholar in the field of Jewish mysticism (the Kabbalah), Gershom Scholem was born to an assimilated German-Jewish family in Berlin and joined the Zionist movement as a young student. He was greatly influenced by the Hebrew writings of Bialik, Zalman Shazar, and S.Y. Agnon.

After first changing his field of studies from mathematics and philosophy to Oriental languages, Scholem produced a doctorate on the Kabbalah. His original research encouraged many scholars to dig deeper into what was then a fairly neglected field. As a result, Jewish mysticism became established as a major discipline.

Scholem joined the staff of the Hebrew University in Jerusalem in 1923. He studied philosophy and the art of bibliography, discovering many previously unknown manuscripts. His papers and writings are taught all over the world, and they have contributed to a better understanding, knowledge, and appreciation of Jewish mysticism.

THEODORE HERZL *(1860–1904)*

Theodore Herzl was the founder of political Zionism, the World Zionist Organization, and the Zionist Congress. Born in Hungary, Herzl was a lawyer but preferred to pursue a career in journalism. The Dreyfus Affair, in which a French Jewish captain was falsely accused of selling military secrets to Germany, brought about a wave of anti-Semitism and prompted Herzl to seek a solution for the persecuted Jewish people. In 1896, he wrote a brochure called *Der Judenstaat (The Jewish State)*, which outlined his program for building an independent Jewish country. *Der Judenstaat* is considered to be the first practical Zionist document that led to the creation of the State of Israel, making Herzl the father of modern Zionism.

Herzl's vision seemed almost too fantastic and as a result fostered a lot of opposition, especially from assimilated Jewish communities that were afraid they might lose the trust of their host countries. He campaigned almost single-handedly among influential European statesmen and in 1897 convened the first World Zionist Congress in Basel, Switzerland. During the congress, the World Zionist Organization was formed, and the seed was planted for a Jewish state.

Not being able to get support for a Jewish state in Palestine from such world leaders as the Turkish Sultan and the German Emperor, Herzl was ready to accept a territory elsewhere. The British government suggested Uganda, but when other Jewish leaders refused to accept any territory but the historic homeland, Herzl withdrew the proposal.

The Uganda affair convinced Herzl and other leaders to concentrate on securing Palestine as a homeland. After visiting the country, he was deeply moved and impressed by its sites and wrote *Alt neuland*, a novel describing a Jewish state in the ancient Land of Israel. His final words in this book, "If you will it, it is no legend," became the slogan of the Zionist movement in years to come. He died in 1904, and his remains were brought to Jerusalem to rest in the mountain named after him, Mount Herzl.

147

HANNAH SENESH *(1921–1944)*

Hannah Senesh is a legendary figure in modern Jewish history. She was born into an assimilated Hungarian Jewish family but became a Zionist in the late 1930s when anti-Semitism arose in her country. She moved to Palestine in 1939 and settled on a kibbutz.

When the news about Hitler's Final Solution reached Palestine, Senesh joined a group of British-trained Haganah (the early Israeli army) members who parachuted into occupied Europe. Their goal was to rescue Allied pilots, organize resistance, and set up a rescue operation for Jews.

A few days before the Germans marched in and occupied Hungary, Senesh parachuted into Yugoslavia and was caught while crossing the border into Hungary. Refusing to give away information, even under torture, she was executed by firing squad. She left a diary that she had written when she was between the ages of thirteen and twenty-two and a few poems written in both Hungarian and Hebrew. Her body was exhumed in 1950, and she was reburied in Israel.

MOSHE DAYAN *(1915–1981)*

One of the best-known Israeli military commanders and statesman, Moshe Dayan was born in Kibbutz Deganya and raised in Moshav Nahalal. He joined the Haganah and during the riots in Palestine from 1936 to 1939 served with the special police force in the Jezreel Valley and in Galilee. Dayan was arrested in 1940 by the British Mandate Government for commanding an illegal Haganah course. After his release from prison, Dayan joined a reconnaissance unit that preceded the British army's invasion of Syria. He lost an eye in an encounter with Vichy forces, and his famous black eyepatch became his trademark.

During the 1948 War of Independence, Dayan commanded the defense of the Jewish settlements, and in 1952 he became the Chief of Operations at the Israel Defense General Headquarters. In this position, he commanded the Israeli Army throughout the Sinai Campaign in 1956.

After leaving the army in 1958, Dayan was elected to the Knesset as a member of the Mapai party and was made Minister of Agriculture. Dayan also conducted a study tour of the Vietnam War, and the diary he wrote during that period became an international best-seller, attracting great attention.

In 1967, he was invited to rejoin the government as the Minister of Defense; he served in this capacity during the Six Day War. After the war, he implemented the liberal military government policy that opened the borders of Israel to Arabs residing in the occupied territories. In his last years, he served as a minister in the opposition Likud party's government under Menachem Begin, which left many members of the Mapai party disappointed.

TEDDY KOLLEK *(1911–   )*

One of the most popular Jewish leaders in the world, Teddy Kollek was born in Vienna and started his political career in the Hehalutz movement in Czechoslovakia, Germany, and England between 1931 and 1934. Kollek moved to Palestine in 1935 and served in the Political Department of the Jewish Agency between 1940 and 1947. He spent part of this time in Istanbul as a contact for the Jewish underground in Europe. Kollek also filled such positions as representative of the Haganah in the United States, Israel's Minister Plenipotentiary in Washington, and Chairman of the Israel Government Tourist Corporation. He also raised funds for the Israel Museum in Jerusalem, of which he was founder and chairman.

Since 1965 he has served as Mayor of Jerusalem, bringing great enthusiasm and charm to this role. Since 1967, when he became the first mayor of the reunified Jerusalem, he has supported the normalization of relations between Jerusalem's Jewish and Arab citizens. Kollek is also the author of various books on Jerusalem.

Government

Israel is a true democracy headed by a president who is elected for five years by the members of the Knesset, the Israeli equivalent of Parliament. His title is honorary, however, and his duties do not resemble the duties of the president of the United States.

Every Israeli citizen, both Jew and Arab, is eligible to vote at the age of eighteen. Each party publishes a list of candidates and the population votes according to party, so that the 120 members of Knesset are voted into office according to the number of mandates won by each party. There is a one percent minimum by which a party can be elected to the Knesset; the total number of seats won is proportionate to the party's percentage of the total vote. (For instance, if a party wins ten percent of the total eligible votes, it will have twelve members at the Knesset. The first twelve candidates that appear on the party's election list then become members of the Knesset.) After an election, the president calls on one of the parties to form a government.

The two largest parties in the country are the (left-leaning) Labor and the (right-leaning) Likud. In the past few years, the number of parties has frequently changed and the shifts in the Israeli political arena have been dramatic, with the religious

The Israeli parliament, the Knesset, is in Jerusalem.

parties playing a key role in forming successive governments. The modus vivendi between left and right has been interrupted in recent years owing to many critical events in the region.

Although Israel has no written constitution, fundamental rights and freedoms are generally protected by law. Israeli law is a blending of different influences, including that of the Ottoman Empire and British Common Law. There are no jury trials in Israel and judges are not elected, but are rather appointed by the president. In personal matters such as divorce, the system of religious courts is still in force. However, even though Israel is a Jewish state, there is no official state religion, so each religion dictates its own rules with respect to personal matters such as marriage and divorce.

The armed forces play a key role in Israeli society. Army service is mandatory for both men and women. At the age of eighteen, young Israelis enter the army— men for three years and women for two. After finishing their term of service, men and women can either choose the Army as a career or be released. Each man in Israel is also required to serve as a reservist for at least thirty days each year. (The number of days increases when there is a military crisis.)

The Israeli Army is one of the most acclaimed armies in the world. It helps to create young people who are strong, mature, and trustworthy. It enables the young Israeli to approach life in a serious and open-eyed way, as a person who has already taken responsibility for defending his country's safety. Army reserve service often causes great disturbances in a person's life, as a reservist must cease his daily routine for a full month or more. But most Israelis, born into these circumstances, see Army service as natural and unavoidable—a responsibility of citizenship.

The Habimah, Israel's national theater company, is based in Tel Aviv.

Culture

150

The phenomenon of the birth of the State of Israel is unique in recent world history. Its growth under special circumstances has given rise to a rich new culture that reflects a new society. Out of the desert grew theater, literature, poetry, music, dance, and various other art forms that have made Israeli arts and artists well known all over the world.

Tiny as it is, Israel has five major theater companies. The internationally acclaimed Habimah, Israel's national theater, began operating as a Hebrew theater in Russia at the beginning of the century, and, upon moving to Israel, established itself in Tel Aviv. The Habimah tours throughout the world, participates in international theater festivals, and produces both new and familiar plays.

Two other theaters exist in Tel Aviv, the Cameri and Neve Tzedek. The Cameri is the Tel Aviv municipal theater, a well-established company that is also internationally acclaimed. Neve Tzedek is a fairly new theater dedicated to performing new Israeli plays and to the development of new Hebrew playwrights. The playhouse is in the Neve Tzedek neighborhood, one of the oldest sections of Tel Aviv.

Haifa Theater and the Be'er Sheva Theater Company have been in existence for twenty years and are based in the cities after which they are named. Jerusalem also has its own company, Hakhan, which performs all over Israel. Almost all of the theaters have exchange programs, which enable them to take their art out of their hometowns and bring it to other cities and communities. In addition to these companies, smaller, experimental groups appear on the scene every year. Some groups survive and some disappear after a season, but together they create a vital, modern, and lively theatrical climate in Israel.

The Israeli Ballet, the only successful classical ballet company in Israel, was founded in 1970. It is the creation of the husband and wife team of Hillel Markman

151

Having recently immigrated to Israel from Tadzhikistan, this father and son are members of the Amalov Family Drummers.

This musical performance by the Hora Jerusalem was staged at Binyaneh Háoomah, the convention center in Jerusalem.

and Berta Yampulski. After years of struggle, the company today is flourishing, performing in Israel and throughout the world, and representing Israel with pride.

The two other dance companies in Israel are modern dance groups: the Bat Sheva Dance Company and the Bat Dor Dance Company. Both are funded largely by grants and fellowships from Israel and abroad. The companies tour each year, performing mostly original works by Israeli choreographers. Another interesting company is the Kol Udmama Dance Company (Sound and Silence). This group combines dancers with normal hearing and dancers who have a partial or total hearing loss. The unusual mixture yields a fascinating performance ensemble that has created a professional, original, and imaginative dance group. The Inbal Dance Company, which is mainly dedicated to preserving authentic Yemenite dance, has also received great admiration both in Israel and worldwide.

Next to the Habimah Theater in Tel Aviv is the Mann Auditorium, home of the Israeli Philharmonic. The orchestra, founded in 1936, is internationally known and highly respected; it is the musical pride of Israel. Leonard Bernstein and Zubin

Mehta, among others, have been associated with this fine group of musicians. The orchestra also travels abroad a few times a year to fulfill the demand for its music. Although the Israeli Philharmonic is not the only orchestra in Israel—there is also the Be'er Sheva Sinfonieta, the Haifa Orchestra, and the Kibbutz Orchestra—it stands as the leading exponent of classical music in Israel.

Young Israel has also produced many fine Hebrew-language writers. In the past few years, a growing number of Israeli writers have been translated into many languages and have acquired fame and recognition from the world's literary communities. Among them are Amos Oz, A.B. Yehoshua, Rachel Eitan, Aharon Appelfeld, and, most recently, David Grossman.

Artists such as Ya'acov Agam and Moshe Kastel have become known worldwide, and their modern, innovative art is displayed in art galleries and museums all over the world.

Israel's universities are famous for the exceptional education they provide and for the scholars that they have produced over the years. The Hebrew University Medical School is a leader in world medicine. The Technion, the Technological Institute of Israel, is a leading technical institute that graduates world-famous engineers and scientists. Tel Aviv, Haifa, and Be'er Sheva universities are newer institutions for higher education in Israel and serve as a resource for young scholars. Tel Aviv University's Rubin Music Academy and the Jerusalem Music Academy are internationally known schools that have introduced such great artists as Yafim Bronfman, Pinchas Zukerman, Pnina Saltzman, and Itzhak Perlman. The Weizmann Institute in Rehovot is not only an agricultural invention center but also a center for scientific research known throughout the world.

And the list grows every day, adding actors, singers, composers, and inventors to the world's leading personalities. The miracle in the desert keeps growing.

153

The Hora Jerusalem Dance Troupe frequently performs at the Binyaneh Háoomah in Jerusalem.

JEWISH ORGANIZATIONS IN NORTH AMERICA

America-Israel Cultural
  Foundation
41 East 42nd Street
Suite 608
New York, NY 10017
(212) 557-1600

American Jewish
  Committee
165 East 56th Street
New York, NY 10022
(212) 751-4000

American Jewish Congress
15 East 84th Street
New York, NY 10028
(212) 879-4500

American Zionist
  Federation
110 East 59th Street
New York, NY 10022
(212) 371-7750

Anti-Defamation League
  of B'nai Brith
823 United Nations Plaza
New York, NY 10017
(212) 490-2525

B'nai Brith Canada
15 Hove Street
Downsview, Ontario
M3H 4Y8
(416) 633-6224

Canadian Foundation for
  Jewish Culture
4600 Bathurst Street
Willowdale, Ontario
M2R 3V2
(416) 635-2883

Canadian Jewish Congress
1590 Dr. Penfield Avenue
Montreal, Quebec
H3G 1C5
(514) 931-7531

Canadian Zionist
  Federation
5250 Decarie Blvd.
Suite 550
Montreal, Quebec
H3X 2H9
(514) 486-9526

Conference of Presidents
  of Major American
  Jewish Organizations
110 East 59th Street
New York, NY 10022
(212) 752-1616

Emunah Women of
  America
7 Penn Plaza
New York, NY 10001
(212) 564-9045

Habonim-Dror
27 West 29th Street
9th Floor
New York, NY 10017
(212) 255-1796

Hadassah
50 West 58th Street
New York, NY 10019
(212) 355-7900

HIAS
200 Park Avenue South
New York, NY 10003
(212) 674-6800

Jewish Reconstructive
  Foundation
Church Road at
  Greenwood Avenue
Wyncota, PA 19095
(215) 887-1988

Rabbinical Council of
  America
275 Seventh Avenue
New York, NY 10001
(212) 807-7888

Union of American Hebrew
  Congregations
838 Fifth Avenue
New York, NY 10021
(212) 249-0100

Union of Councils for
  Soviet Jews
1819 H Street NW
Suite 230
Washington, DC 20006
(202) 775-9770

United Jewish Appeal
99 Park Avenue
Suite 300
New York, NY 10016
(212) 818-9100

United Synagogues of
  America
155 Fifth Avenue
New York, NY 10010
(212) 353-9539

World Jewish Congress
501 Madison Avenue
17th Floor
New York, NY 10022
(212) 755-5770

PHOTOGRAPHY CREDITS